Loretta Santini

UMBRIA

ART AND HISTORY

CENTRO STAMPA EDITORIALE

plurigraf

PERSEUS

INDEX

© Copyright by CASA EDITRICE PERSEUS-PLURIGRAF
Published and printed by Centro Stampa Editoriale, Sesto Fiorentino, (Fi).

INTRODUCTION

Umbria has been described in many different ways: Umbria, the heart of Italy; green Umbria; Umbria, the land of saints and warriors. But which of these is the real definition? All of them, perhaps. This delightful region in fact does form the heart of Italy, not only because of its central geographic location, but also because it is a meeting-point for customs and characteristics peculiar to the whole of Italy, belonging to both its past and present civilizations. It is also green, because in the valleys and endless series of hills and mountains that form its scenery, greenery and woodland prevail with unchallenged supremacy. And it is too a land of saints and warriors and - we would add - of artists. Suffice it to mention the names of St. Francis of Assisi, patron saint of Italy, St. Benedict of Norcia, St. Clare, St. Valentine, and St. Rita; among the region's condottieri, we would mention Erasmo of Narni, known as Gattamelata, Braccio da Montone known as Fortebraccio, Piccinino and Bartolomeo d'Alviano. And of Umbria's artists we would remember Perugino, Pinturicchio, Fra' Bevignate da Perugia, Gattapone and Piermatteo d'Amelia, not to mention the other famous artists who painted there, first and foremost Giotto, followed by Benozzo Gozzoli, Raphael, Sangallo, Signorelli and Vignola.

Umbria is all this, and much more. It is a land in which the countryside is gentle and restful, a land in which both ancient and medieval civilization flourished. It is a land of delightful towns like Perugia, Gubbio, Assisi, Spoleto, Todi and Orvieto, which attract the visitor with the

beauty of their buildings and monuments. Besides them, a throng of smaller towns and villages are scattered over Umbria's green hills, equally full of the medieval atmosphere which is so characteristic of all Umbrian towns and makes them so picturesque. The charm of these towns lies in the tranquillity and silence of their centres, in their typical medieval appearance, with narrow winding streets, stairways, arches and porticoes, and low houses built side by side and irregular in structure so as to follow the conformation of the ground, or even emerging from the bare rock on which they stand.

Umbria is above all the land of a hundred medieval towns, often defined as a "town-region". It is a kind and simple land, but at the same time is austere and strong; it is mystical and gentle but also proud. It is a region in which past and present live together in singular harmony: the history, customs, traditions, culture and art of the past are still alive and present today in its towns and in its people.

At the same time, it has responded to the economical, social and cultural ferments of modern civilization, and kept pace with them, but thanks to the nature and influence of its past, it has avoided the excessive upheavals that have left their mark on so many other cities and regions of Italy. It is perhaps for this reason that Umbria remains a quiet and unspoiled region with a restful, peaceful atmosphere, and this is true of its more modern towns also. In its picturesque hill-top villages or on the top of its mountains, the soul is soothed by its verdant landscape, its magnificent views, and its many lovely buildings, churches and works of art.

GEOGRAPHY

Umbria covers an area of approximately 8,500 square kilometres. Its neighbouring regions are Tuscany, the Marches and Latium, and it is the only region of the Italian peninsula to have no coastline. It is divided into

two provinces: Perugia and Terni. Its name derives from one of the oldest Italic peoples, the Umbrians, who settled in a large part of central Italy in prehistoric times but after the advent of the Etruscans limited themselves to the left bank of the Tiber. Umbria kept the same name in Roman times but this referred to a much larger area than it does today. Umbria was formally adopted as the name of the region after the unification of Italy (1861); at the time it included part of the territory of Rieti and consisted of only one province, Perugia.

The second province, Terni, was created in 1927 after the town of the same name had come to assume considerable importance following an intense and rapid process of industrial development, which began in 1882 with the establishment of an armaments factory and continued with the building of a steel works two years later, leading to urban and population growth. Umbria is mainly a mountainous and hilly region, with the highest peaks of the Apennines between Umbria and the Marches not rising above 1500 metres.

There is little flat land in the region, and this is generally situated in the river valleys: the valley of the Tiber which runs across the region from north to south in the west, and the Umbrian valley to the east. There are also smaller valleys and basins surrounded by mountains scattered throughout the region.

The main river in the region is the Tiber, into which almost all the other Umbrian rivers flow: the Nera, the Chiascio, the Topino and the Paglia. The two main lakes are Trasimeno, north-west of Perugia, and Piediluco, near Terni. A unique feature of the Umbrian landscape is the spectacular Marmore Waterfalls (Cascata delle Marmore).

HISTORY

As already mentioned, this land was inhabited in ancient times by the Umbrians, an Italic people and distinct ethnic group with its own language, an offshoot of the Indo-European family, of which evidence has come down to us today in the form of the "Eugubine Tablets", a series of bronze inscriptions kept in the Palazzo dei Consoli at Gubbio. The Umbrians settled on the land situated on the left bank of the Tiber, from Gubbio to Todi, Gualdo Tadino, Terni and Narni. The right bank of the Tiber was inhabited by the Etruscans, who occupied part of the Umbrians' territory and turned Perugia and Orvieto into their main centres.

The expansion of Rome began in the 4th century B.C. and, although the Umbrians and Etruscans put up strong resistance and even joined forces against their common enemy, the Roman advance proved increasingly difficult to resist, and the whole region was completely subjugated by the 3rd century B.C.. Roman civilization thus came to flourish in the region, the evidence of which still exists today in the form of numerous monuments. But the unmistakeable sign of the growing importance of Rome and of Umbria itself was the construction of major roads like the Via Salaria and in particular the Via Flaminia, which runs through the whole of the region.

On the fall of the Roman Empire, Umbria was invaded by the Goths and Lombards. The latter created the Duchy of Spoleto which, from the 8th century onwards, came under the dominion of the emergent State of the Church, whose sovereignty imposed itself in the 12th century under Pope Innocent III.

At the same time, a great number of city-states sprang up throughout the region, giving rise to the flourishing cultural and artistic development that has given a unique and indelible stamp to Umbrian towns which has been preserved, unchanged, down to our own day.

Politically, however, the age of the city-states was an age of strife and continuous battles for independence; Perugia, Assisi, Gubbio and many other towns in the region, large and small, were the theatre of innumerable disputes and wars, sometimes against one another and sometimes against the Papacy.

From the point of view of religion Umbria, which had been converted to Christianity at a very early date and in the 6th century had been the birthplace of St. Benedict of Norcia founder of the Benedictine Order stood out during the Middle Ages for the many saints it produced, in particular the great St. Francis of Assisi. For this reason it has been called a "mystic land".

The 14th and 15th centuries witnessed the foundation of a number of Signorie, or feudal lordships, at Foligno, Città di Castello, Todi and Perugia, where one of the most important universities of the time flourished. But the Signorie were limited in their territorial and political development by the increasingly predominant presence of the Papacy which, from 1500 onwards, with the conquest of Perugia, laid down the foundations for an unchallenged supremacy which was to last, practically, until the region was incorporated in the Kingdom of Italy in 1861.

UMBRIA: A TOWN-REGION CULTURE AND ART

Umbria today presents on the whole a homogeneous face, probably because there has been no great disparity in tradition, history or culture within the region, despite the complexity of the factors that have formed its civilization.

Its relatively small population (some 800,000 inhabitants in all), the balanced distribution of economic enterprise in the various towns (hence its definition as a town-region), its rational incorporation in the industrial development of the nation and at the same time its conscious promotion of handicrafts and of all those forms of culture and craftsmanship which have formed the social and economic substratum of Umbria for centuries all these factors have ensured that the region has maintained its own distinct character and, at the same time a human face.

Hence the survival, or rather the continuing life, of a myriad of medieval towns, large and small, with their unaltered appearance, the exceptional beauty of their monuments and churches, and the picturesque quality of their streets and houses. Hence too, the continuing flourishing, often to high artistic standards, of handicrafts in pottery, copper, wrought iron and wood, in many Umbrian towns such as Deruta, Gubbio, Orvieto, Assisi, Città di Castello, Todi and Perugia, to mention just a few.

The continuation of the past is also guaranteed by the many historical festivals and contests which take place each year: the Race of the Candles (Corsa dei Ceri) at Gubbio, the Jousting Tournament (Quintana) at Foligno, the May Day Festival (Calendimaggio) at Assisi, the Water Festival (Festa delle Acque) at Marmore and Piediluco and the Ring Race (Corsa dell'Anello) at Narni. These and other events are not just revived to commemorate the past, but are live traditions which have been followed for centuries. Nor must we forget that in addition to these there are annual religious festivals such as the Corpus Christi Procession at Orvieto, the festivities at Assisi to commemorate St. Francis, St. Clare and the Holy Week, celebrations at Cascia to commemorate St. Rita, at Norcia to commemorate St. Benedict, and at Terni on St. Valentine's Day, in honour of lovers.

Numerous cultural and artistic events of the greatest interest also take place in Umbria each year, the major ones being the Festival of the Two Worlds at Spoleto, and the Umbria Jazz Festival. In addition to these, there are countless musical festivals, theatre seasons, exhibitions and conferences. In every corner of Umbria there is in fact a cultural and historical substratum that continually comes to the surface and forms an integral part of the life and customs of the population: it is this that in large part characterizes the region and distinguishes it as a land in which past and present are united by the sensitivity of its inhabitants, by its proud and austere civilization, by its simplicity.

Umbrian cuisine, too, bears the mark of this culture. It is not perhaps remarkable for a large number of its own original dishes, but it can boast excellent regional products such as olive oil, wine and a variety of pork sausages, salamis and hams (for which the people of Norcia are especially renowned).

Above all, Umbrian cooking is homely, traditional and healthy: tasty and easily digestible at the same time. Pasta is often home-made, bread and biscuits are baked in wood-fired ovens, and there is a wide variety of delicious local cheeses and locally produced meats, such as baby lamb, kid and pork, as well as fish. A much-used ingredient in all Umbrian dishes is the high-quality olive oil widely produced throughout the region.

Excellent black truffles are found in several areas, especially around Norcia.

Even in its cuisine, in Umbria the past lives in the present, and the present is enhanced by its links with the past. This is the true nature, the real essence, of Umbria.

PERUGIA

"*Augusta Perusia*" was the name given to this ancient city by the Romans when the emperor Augustus rebuilt it after his troops had successfully besieged and in large part destroyed it during the civil war against Anthony. Before occupation by the Romans, Perugia had originally been a settlement of the Umbrians and then of the Etruscans who had occupied the right bank of the Tiber and of whose civiliza-

tion splendid remains are still visible. Besieged and destroyed by Totila the Goth in the 6th century, Perugia became an independent city-state in the 11th century, when it was embellished with magnificent buildings and assumed the appearance it still retains today. Involved in the political strife of the time, Perugia was tormented by various struggles against the neighbouring city-states of Gubbio and As-

sisi. Later it was ruled by various lords, including the Baglioni, and then came under the control of the papal legates. The latter consolidated their position under the Farnese Pope Paul III, who was responsible for erecting the fortress known as the Rocca Paolina, the stronghold of the Papal States. Papal rule continued virtually unchallenged until the period of the Risorgimento and the formation of the King-

dom of Italy in 1861, apart from brief interludes during the Napoleonic occupation (late 18th century) and during the constitution of the Roman Republic, in which papal power in the town was temporarily suspended.

Perugia is undoubtedly one of the most interesting and charming cities in Italy. The number and beauty of its monuments, its churches and civic buildings make it an artistic centre of major importance. It contains numerous examples of Etruscan, Roman, Romanesque and Gothic architecture, and of sculpture and paintings by famous artists.

The city is built on a hill-top some 500 metres high, spread over its slopes in the form of a star. The oldest part of the city dates from Etruscan times, and is still partially situated within the mighty walls dating from that period, in which there are various gateways: the Arch of Augustus, the Porta Sole, the Porta della Mandorla, the Porta Marzia, the Porta Trasimeno and Cornea (or Sant'Ercolano). Other arches affording entry into the town were added in Roman and medieval times, as the city gradually extended beyond its original size.

Today Perugia preserves the structure of its past almost unaltered, with its steep alleys and stairways, its beautiful old buildings, its picturesque corners, and its magnificent panoramic views over the countryside below.

PIAZZA QUATTRO NOVEMBRE AND THE FOUNTAIN (FONTANA MAGGIORE)

One of the most beautiful squares in Italy, Piazza Quattro Novembre marks the centre of Perugia. Surrounded by elegant buildings of great interest, at its centre stands the marvellous *Fountain* (Fontana Maggiore).

Designed by Nicola and Giovanni Pisano and Fra Bevignate of Perugia in the second half of the 13th century, the fountain consists of two polygonal basins, placed one on top of the other on a raised, circular platform made up of steps. In the middle of the upper basin a column supports a bronze bowl and sculpture of three nymphs.

Of particular interest are the sculptures carved on the two basins by Nicola and Giovanni Pisano. The months of the year, the signs of the zodiac, the liberal arts and biblical scenes are portrayed in the panels of the lower basin, while the panels of the upper basin are plain but are separated by 24 statues of biblical, mythological and historical figures and saints.

Piazza IV Novembre.
Palazzo dei Priori, Fountain.

CATHEDRAL OF SAN LORENZO

In the same square, situated at the top of a flight of steps, we can admire one of the side walls of the 14th century Cathedral of San Lorenzo, beautifully decorated with a geometric motif in white and pink marble along the whole of its lower part. The Crucifix placed high up on the wall, protected behind glass, was chosen by the Perugians to protect their city in their struggle against the Papacy to resist the levying of a tax on salt by Paul III in 1539 (the so-called salt war). A fine bronze statue of Julius III, the work of the Perugian sculptor Vincenzo Danti, stands on a pedestal at the side of the Cathedral. The 15th century pulpit decorated with mosaics, situated close to the Cathedral entrance, is also of interest. Of note, although it is not part of the Cathedral, is the elegant *Loggia of Braccio Fortebraccio*, dating from the 15th century. The façade of the Cathedral, redesigned in the baroque period, faces onto the neighbouring Piazza Danti.

The interior of the Cathedral is of considerable interest and contains precious works of art. We should mention in particular the *Chapel of the Holy Ring* (Cappella del Santo Anello) in which a ring considered by tradition to be the betrothal ring of the Virgin is preserved in a precious Tabernacle of carved gold, the *Chapel of San Bernardino* (Cappella di San Bernardino), the beautiful wooden choir stalls in the presbytery made by Giuliano da Majano and Domenico del Tasso, and several valuable paintings and sculptures.

The adjoining *Cathedral Museum* (Museo dell'Opera del Duomo) contains some fine paintings, precious documents and ancient manuscripts.

Loggia of Braccio Fortebraccio.

Interior of the Cathedral of San Lorenzo.

Below: Piazza IV Novembre, Fountain, Cathedral of San Lorenzo.

PALAZZO DEI PRIORI

On the opposite side of the square, facing the Cathedral, stands the magnificent Palazzo dei Priori, which extends along the bustling main street, Corso Vannucci. Built between the late 12th and early 13th century, it represents one of the finest and most elegant examples of Gothic architecture in Italy.

The façade looking onto the square, of more austere appearance than the rest of the building, is distinguished by a flight of steps leading up to an impressive doorway through which one enters the Chamber of Notaries (Sala dei Notari) and by a portico occupying the site of the former Church of San Severo. Over the portal, placed on brackets, are the symbols of Perugia: the griffin and the lion (the latter indicating that the city was Guelph). The side of the Palazzo dei Priori which runs along Corso Vannucci - the other side flanks a narrow alley and is incorporated among other medieval buildings - is notable for its unusual undulating wall which follows the course of the street, for its series of handsome Gothic mullioned windows and for its lavishly and elegantly decorated *doorway*. This magnificent exterior, with its delicate polychromy and interlaced decoration, provides a fitting focal point for the centre of Perugia as a whole.

The interior of the Palazzo dei Priori houses the austere and impressive *Sala dei Notari* (Chamber of Notaries), of vast proportions, supported by massive arches and decorated with coats of arms and a series of frescoes along its walls portraying religious subjects, legends and *"Stories from the Old and New Testament"*.

Corso Vannucci.

National Gallery of Umbria

The Gallery houses the most important and most complete collection of Umbrian painting in Italy, embracing a period ranging from the early 13th to the late 16th century.

There is also a section with 17th and 18th century paintings and the Caratoli Collection.

The Gallery occupies part of the Palazzo dei Priori and has recently been reorganized so that visitors can follow a route which illustrates the course of Italian painting and sculpture and that of its major artists.

The Gallery boasts sculptures by Arnolfo di Cambio and a number of paintings by Perugino (Pietro Vannucci, born in 1446 at Città della Pieve, a small town near Perugia), whose art is characterized by graceful lines, soft and harmonious colouring and a sweet and gentle atmosphere which was to have a deep influence on his pupil Raphael.

Of the most beautiful of his paintings on display we may mention the "Adoration of the Magi", "The Miracles of St. Bernardino", the "Dead Christ", a Madonna and a "Pietà". Many artists of the 13th and 14th centuries are also represented in the Gallery, including Duccio di Buoninsegna, Taddeo di Bartolo, Salimbeni and especially Beato Angelico, here represented by a magnificent "Madonna and Child".

We may also admire Benozzo Gozzoli's "Flagellation", an interesting polyptych by Piero della Francesca and a series of works by the Umbrian painters Benedetto Bonfigli and Pinturicchio, who is particularly well represented with an ample selection of his art.

One of the rooms next to the Gallery houses a collection dedicated to the history of Perugia, with documents, maps, street plans, coats of arms etc.

Chamber of Notaries.

Madonna and Child - Duccio di Buoninsegna.

The Banner of the Annunziata - Niccolò Alunno.

The Adoration of the Magi - Perugino.

Below: Madonna, Child and Saints - Benozzo Gozzoli.

Madonna, Child and Saints - Domenico di Bartolo.

Dead Christ - attributed to Raphael.

Polyptych by Piero della Francesca.

Predella from the Polyptych of the Dominicans - Beato Angelico.

Madonna, Child and Saints - Perugino.

CHAMBER OF THE COLLEGE OF MERCHANTS AND COUNTING HOUSE (SALA DEL COLLEGIO DELLA MERCANZIA COLLEGIO DEL CAMBIO).

These two chambers are situated on the ground floor of the Palazzo dei Priori, access to them being through a doorway on Corso Vannucci. The former, completely panelled in wood, was used for meetings of the College of Merchants and the latter as a counting-house for money-changers. The Collegio del Cambio consists of two rooms, an anteroom and the counting chamber itself (a kind of chamber of commerce), and is one of the most significant examples of Italian Renaissance art. The entire surface of its walls is decorated with a series of frescoes by Perugino representing the great heroes of antiquity, together with personifications of the virtues, scenes from the Gospel, and the major deities of ancient Greece. There is also a self-portrait by the artist.

Right: Pietro Vannucci, known as Perugino - Self-portrait.
Below left: Page from a 14th century illuminated manuscript.
Below right: Chapel of St. John the Baptist - Giannicola di Paolo.

Above: Chamber of the College of Merchants.

Below: Counting chamber.

CHURCH OF SAN DOMENICO (ST. DOMINIC'S)
NATIONAL ARCHAEOLOGICAL MUSEUM OF UMBRIA

The Church of San Domenico has 14th century origins: its exterior, though rebuilt by Maderno in the 17th century, is imposing and austere, due in part to its somewhat irregular architectural features.

Its interior, too, is impressive and contains a number of precious works of art: handsome 15th century wooden choir-stalls, several paintings of the Umbrian school, and above all a beautiful sepulchral monument to Pope Benedict XI, attributed to some of the most illustrious sculptors of the 14th century, including Giunta Pisano, Arnolfo di Cambio and Lorenzo Maitani.

The apse of the church is remarkable for its huge stained glass window of brilliant hues. Next to the church is the *National Archaeological Museum of Umbria*, which houses an important collection of prehistoric, Etruscan and Roman objects and sculptures from Perugia and other Umbrian towns.

The Museum, which houses the donation of the Friggeri family (end of the 18th century), has been considerably enlarged by the addition of other collections and newly excavated finds from necropolises and other archaeological sites in the region.

It is divided into sections containing prehistoric, Etruscan and Roman objects; the date and place of origin are given for each exhibit.

Among the pieces on display in the Museum is the Cippo Perugino (Perugian Stone), with one of the longest Etruscan inscriptions to have been passed down to us from Etruscan times.

National Archaeological Museum of Umbria. Cippo Perugino (Perugian Stone).

Church of San Domenico.

CHURCH OF SAN PIETRO (ST. PETER'S)

On entering Perugia by the Porta San Costanzo and taking the Borgo XX Giugno, we pass, on the left, the *Frontone Gardens*, laid out on top of the town walls erected by Braccio Fortebraccio in the 15th century. Here there is also a small 18th century *amphitheatre*, while a little further on, to the right, is one of Perugia's most beautiful and important religious buildings: the *church of San Pietro*, distinguished by its slender pointed bell-tower. Built in the 10th century by a Perugian nobleman who later became a Benedictine monk, the church has a pleasing 17th century courtyard in front of it. Its interior, of great architectural beauty, contains an enormous number of sculptures and paintings of significance; we would mention a series of small pictures of saints painted by Perugino, a beautiful marble tabernacle sculpted by Mino da Fiesole, an ornate 16th century high altar with marble and bronze decorations, and superb wooden choir-stalls round the semicircle of the apse. The choir-stalls are a masterpiece of wood carving and marquetry and may perhaps be considered the most beautiful and precious of all choir-stalls to be found in Italy. From a terrace situated behind the choir a magnificent view can be enjoyed of the countryside stretching as far as Assisi. The former Benedictine monastery adjoining the church now houses the Faculty of Agriculture of Perugia University.

CHURCH OF SAN FRANCESCO AL PRATO (ST. FRANCIS'S) ORATORY OF SAN BERNARDINO

From Corso Vannucci, making our way through the vaulted passage under the Palazzo dei Priori, we find ourselves in *Via dei Priori*, one of the most picturesque streets in Perugia, lined with medieval houses and churches.

At the top of the street is the charming 13th century *church of Sant'Agata*, followed by the 17th century *San Filippo Neri*, magnificent in its architecture and proudly situated on top of a high flight of steps. We continue down the steep Via dei Priori, noting the picturesque side streets that open out from it, with their unusual names. After passing the handsome tower known as the *Torre degli Sciri*, we come to another charming corner of medieval Perugia: the square of the *Madonna della Luce* in which the little Renaissance church of the same name and an ancient Etruscan archway known as Porta Trasimeno are situated. Via dei Priori eventually leads into a large airy square with two churches: *San Francesco* and San Bernardino. The former, the larger of the two, is of 13th century origins, but has undergone numerous alterations and restorations. The latter - the *Oratory of San Bernardino* to call it by its proper name - is notable for its delightful multi-coloured exterior, designed by Agostino di Duccio in the mid-15th century on the spot where St. Bernardino, a follower of St. Francis, liked to preach. On the façade, decorated with coloured marble and terracotta, is a large central doorway with a tympanum above. The two pillars on either side of the archway, decorated with niches and sculptures, become more distant as they move upwards to correct an optical illusion by which the building would seem to become narrower towards the top. The interior of the church is of interest too. The Academy of Fine Arts is now housed in the former Convent adjoining the church.

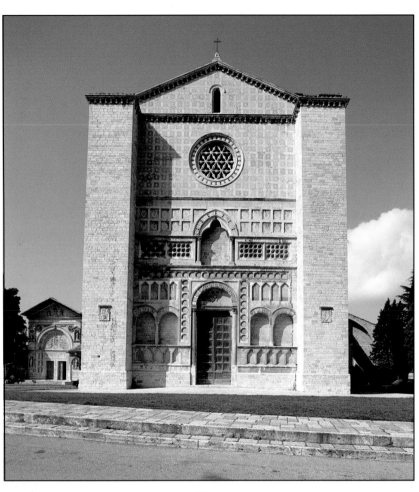

PIAZZA MATTEOTTI

Piazza Matteotti runs parallel with Piazza IV Novembre and Corso Vannucci. It is lined with beautiful buildings, including the *Palazzo dell'Università Vecchia* (Old University Building), with its windows in the form of a cross, dating from the 15th century and seat of the old university, and the splendid *Palazzo del Capitano del Popolo* dating from the second half of the 15th century, distinguished by its elegant mullioned windows with two and three lights.

FORTRESS OF POPE PAUL III (ROCCA PAOLINA)

From the centre of Perugia we descend along the steep Via Marzia which leads to the gate known as the *Porta Marzia*. Dating from the 2nd century B.C., it was incorporated into the walls of Pope Paul III's Fortress - the Rocca Paolina - by the architect

Church of San Francesco al Prato.

Below: Oratory of San Bernardino.

Piazza Matteotti.

Fortress and Lomellina Fountain.

Antonio da Sangallo the Younger who dismantled and rebuilt it a few metres from its original location. It is now the entrance to the *Rocca Paolina*, the stronghold erected by the Farnese Pope Paul III after the Papal States had quelled the resistance of the Perugians during the salt war and succeeded in reinforcing their authority over the town. The fortress came to occupy a whole medieval quarter consisting of noble houses, churches and streets, and was later incorporated in a powerful system of walls and bastions which represented both symbolically and in concrete form the undisputable power of the Church. Particularly fascinating and unforgettable is a visit inside the fortress, following Via Baglioni and looking down at the historic buildings under its battlements. The thick shadow, the picturesque corners, the splendid views through the slits in the fortress walls, everything contributes to creating a unique impression: the past seems to have been frozen indefinitely and to be jealously guarded behind those massive ramparts. It is almost a city within a city, its treasure, its past, its memories, its beauty.

The Rocca Paolina now contains an escalator which links the lower part of Perugia to the centre of the town, and it is used for important exhibitions.

ETRUSCAN ARCH (OR ARCH OF AUGUSTUS) AND PALAZZO GALLENGA

We are now in another of the most important and characteristic spots in Perugia, Piazza Braccio Fortebraccio, which may be approached from several directions; we may either proceed down the steep Via Bartolo which descends from Piazza IV Novembre, flanked by a series of medieval houses, or we may follow Via Battisti, which skirts the impressive *Etruscan circle of walls* made of huge square blocks of stone, affording fine panoramic views of part of the town and the surrounding countryside. In Piazza Fortebraccio stands the *Palazzo Gallenga Stuart*, an elegant and austere 18th century building which now houses the University for Foreigners (Università degli Stranieri). Perugia, which has a long cultural tradition and has been a centre for studies since the 14th century, created this University at the beginning of this century with a view to the diffusion of the Italian language and literature in the world and to facilitate and foster cultural exchanges between different countries and civilizations.

Close by, in the same square, what is commonly considered as the main monument in the town is located: the *Etruscan Arch* or Arch of Augustus. Powerful and proud, imposing in size and in the solidity of its structure, austere in the iron-grey colour of its stonework, it was the northern entrance to the old Etruscan city and also its most important gate. It was restored by the emperor Augustus in the 1st century A.D.. The graceful fountain below and the elegant loggia above were added in the 16th century.

Above: Palazzo Gallenga Stuart which now houses the University for Foreigners.

Below: Etruscan Arch (or Arch of Augustus).

HYPOGEUM OF THE VOLUMNI (IPOGEO DEI VOLUMNI)

Situated close to Perugia on the road leading to Ponte San Giovanni, the *Hypogeum of the Volumni* is one of the largest, most complete and most interesting examples of Etruscan tombs known to us. It was the family burial vault of the Volumni, a noble family of the 2nd century B.C., who, in the Etruscan fashion, wished to give their abode in the after-life the structure and character of a real house as if to prove the continuity of life in the hereafter.

The hypogeum consists of an entrance-hall and, down a flight of steps, an atrium, a tablinum and various surrounding cubicula and rooms. A large collection of sandstone cinerary urns and a variety of grave goods for use by the dead were found in the rooms. There are numerous inscriptions, paintings and bas-relief sculptures in the various tombs. Undoubtedly the most interesting part of the hypogeum is the tablinum (corresponding to the room which served as a study in Roman houses), in which the finest tombs are located. In this room, a group of 7 cinerary urns were found, in which the urn belonging to Arunte Volumnio (as indicated in the inscription) stands out. The statue of the head of the family lies on a draped couch; two powerful figures are carved beneath it representing the genii of death. Beside it there are two other tombs belonging to other members of the family, including the daughter of Arunte. Other Etruscan tombs have been found in the area surrounding Perugia.

Though just as interesting, none is as complex in structure as the Hypogeum of the Volumni. The tombs of San Manno, Villa Sperandio and Bettona are, however, worth mentioning.

Cinerary urn of Arunte Volumnio d'Aulo (2nd century B.C.).

LAKE TRASIMENO

A charming legend recounts how Trasimene, son of the king of Tyrrhenian Lydia, on landing on the western coast of Italy, ventured inland in order to hunt.

He thus came to this enchanting place where he fell desperately in love with Agilla, nymph of the lake.

He married her and in order to follow her, plunged with her into the waters which were then named after him. Lake Trasimeno (45 kilometres in circumference, 7 metres deep) is the largest lake in Central Italy. Roughly circular in shape, its shores are surrounded by rolling green hills and dotted with charming little bathing and tourist resorts.

There are three small islands in the lake: Isola Maggiore, Isola Minore and Isola Polvese.

All are of interest and easily accessible from various points on the shore, thanks to a rapid and efficient ferry-boat service. Lake Trasimeno is famous in history for the battle named after it, fought between Hannibal and the Romans in 217 B.C., and ending with the crushing defeat of the latter. The blood shed in the battle is still remembered in the names of the village of Sanguineto and of the River Ossala.

PASSIGNANO SUL TRASIMENO

This is an important lakeside resort, situated in part along the shores of the lake, where there are tourist facilities, and in part over the slopes of the hill behind, where the older and more characteristic part of the town, with its predominantly medieval appearance, is to be found. In fact the old part still preserves almost intact its circle of walls and its picturesque maze of alleys, stairways, arches, little squares and houses, which create a charming and suggestive atmosphere. There is easy access by ferry-boat to the islands in the lake from Passignano, and its bathing establishments have undergone considerable development recently.

The three islands of the lake - *Isola Maggiore, Isola Minore* and *Isola Polvese* - are very beautiful. Isola Polvese, the largest of the three, is a public park, while on Isola Maggiore there is a picturesque fishing village which has kept its 15th century

appearance and character and boasts two interesting buildings, Villa Isabella and the church of San Michele Arcangelo. Lacework of a high quality is a local handicraft.

Other lake-side towns include *San Feliciano* and the picturesque village

of *Monte San Biagio*.

Castel Rigone, an enchanting little hill-town 650 metres high, is notable for its panoramic views over the lake, its interesting centre full of character, and a noteworthy Renaissance church, the Madonna dei Miracoli (Madonna of the Miracles) which contains works of art of interest.

After Passignano, we come to *Tuoro sul Trasimeno*. On the road between Lake Trasimeno and Perugia, the towns of Magione and Corciano are to be found.

The main feature of *Magione* is the massive structure of its stupendous *Abbey* or Castle of the Knights of Malta, built at the beginning of the 15th century on the site of an old Benedictine monastery.

Corciano has preserved the medieval appearance of its historical centre near the Castle, with its towers and walls. The church of Santa Maria contains paintings by Bonfigli and Perugino. A number of artistic and cultural events take place in the town.

Above: Foreshortening.
Below: Passignano sul Trasimeno.

CASTIGLIONE DEL LAGO

A bustling town on the western shores of Lake Trasimeno, Castiglione del Lago is built on a small promontory on the lake. If we look a little more closely at the shape of this promontory we may easily see that it once formed another island, but the gradual diminution of the lake led to the formation of the strip of land that now joins it to the mainland. The area was inhabited from a very early date, as testified by the interesting Etruscan and Roman remains found nearby. In the Middle Ages it was the site of an important castle, the control of which was contested by various lords, including the Marchesi della Corgna whose palace and imposing castle can still be admired today. The town later became part of the Papal States.

A visit round the little town shows us several interesting buildings, such as the *Church of the Maddalena* in which a fresco is preserved that was probably painted by the young Raphael or, in any case, by one of Perugino's pupils. Also worth seeing is the Ducal Palace (Palazzo Ducale) which belonged to the Marchesi della Cogna and is now used as the town hall, and which contains frescoes depicting mythological scenes and historical episodes mostly dating from the 16th century.

The most important monument of the town is, however, the Castle, a massive and austere building, still surrounded by its fine circle of walls and fortified towers. Remains of the walkway which linked it to the Ducal Palace are still visible.

At the edge of the town, tourist and sport facilities are to be found, in addition to a lovely beach on the shores of the Trasimeno.

CITTÀ DELLA PIEVE

In a lovely position overlooking the Chiana Valley, Città della Pieve was first an Etruscan then a Roman town (when it was called Castrum Plebis). Perugino, the artist who brought fame and prestige to Umbrian Renaissance painting, was born here.

He left numerous paintings in his birthplace: "The Adoration of the Magi" (in the church of Santa Maria dei Bianchi, where he also left several signed autographs); "The Deposition of Christ" (in the church of Santa Maria dei Servi), a "Madonna, Child and Saints" and "The Baptism of Christ" (in the Cathedral); and "St. Anthony the Abbot and other Saints" (in the church of Sant'Antonio Abate).

The town has largely preserved its medieval structure. The 12th century Cathedral is of interest, with its Gothic features, and the churches of San Francesco, dating from the 13th century, and Sant'Agostino.

The splendid 14th century Fortress with its handsome towers and Palazzo Bandini designed by Galeazzo Alessi are worthy of note.

PANICALE

This medieval village has kept its original appearance and still preserves intact its old houses, walls, buildings, gateways and streets.

The central square is enhanced by Palazzo Pretorio and a pretty fountain.

The *church of San Michele* is very beautiful and the church of San Sebastiano is of great interest, containing the notable "Martyrdom of St. Sebastian" and a Madonna by Perugino. We may also mention the *church of Sant'Agostino* and the town walls with its towers which jealously guard the rocky hill on which Panicale stands.

There are magnificent views from the terrace in Piazza Vittorio.

UMBERTIDE

A town of ancient origin - in Roman times it was known as Pitulum - it flourished particularly from the 10th century onwards.

It boasts several monuments: the 15th century *church of Santa Maria*, the *church of Santa Croce*, with its beautiful "Deposition" painted by Signorelli, and the *Fortress*. The delightful *Castello di Civitella Ranieri* is to be found nearby.

Umbertide is famous for its ceramics factory.

Panicale - General view.

CITTÀ DI CASTELLO

During the Middle Ages and Renaissance, Città di Castello was one of the most important cultural and artistic centres; famous artists, including Raphael, Signorelli, Perugino, Pinturicchio, Della Robbia, Sangallo, Rosso Fiorentino and Vasari, worked there.

It held a prestigious place in the arts of printing and ceramics.

Its most important monuments include the Gothic *Palazzo Comunale*, the 16th century *Palazzo Vitelli* (designed by Antonio Sangallo the Younger and decorated in part by Vasari), and the *Cathedral*, begun in the 11th century and altered several times, containing a splendid "Transfiguration of Christ" by Rosso Fiorentino and, in the Treasury, precious church furnishings and objects.

The *Palazzo della Podestà*, the *church of San Domenico* (St. Dominic's) and other religious buildings are also worthy of note.

The impressive *Pinacoteca* (Picture Gallery) contains the largest collection of Umbrian art after the National Gallery in Perugia. Its most important works include terracotta sculptures by the Della Robbia family and paintings by Signorelli, Pomarancio, Raphael, Raffaellino del Colle and Ghirlandaio.

Città di Castello is also the birthplace of a great innovator in contemporary painting, Burri, most of whose work is kept in a special museum in the town.

Above: Umbertide - Fortress.

Below: Città di Castello - Round Bell-tower (12th century) and Cathedral.

GUBBIO

Gubbio is known as "the most beautiful of medieval towns". Of all the towns in Umbria richly endowed with the heritage of their past, with their own special character, and with great charm thanks to their monuments and atmosphere, Gubbio is undoubtedly the one that has kept its medieval appearance most intact. Its streets, monuments, churches and houses are still perfectly preserved, the testimony of a glorious period in history, the Middle Ages, when Gubbio was not only economically prosperous, but politically powerful and unwavering in the defence of its freedom as a city-state.

Gubbio was originally founded by the Umbrians, an ancient people who settled on the land on the left of the Tiber. Evidence of exceptional importance belonging to this interesting Italic civilization is kept in the town: the *Eugubine Tablets*, a unique document in the Umbrian language recording a series of religious regulations and rituals. Coins belonging to the same people are preserved, together with the Tablets, in the Palazzo dei Consoli. Archaeological finds of the same period also exist in the area surrounding Gubbio.

Later occupied by the Romans, Gubbio changed its name from Ikuvium to Iguvium. During the Roman period too the town achieved a certain degree of importance, as demonstrated by the theatres and temples which were built there (the most important of the theatres survives virtually intact). Even the existing town layout recalls the original Roman street plan with its straight streets lying parallel to or crossing over each other, spread over the side of Mt. Ingino. It was over this typically Roman urban layout that the medieval town was developed.

After the fall of the Roman Empire

Palazzo dei Consoli.

and the barbarian invasions (the town was sacked by the Goths in the 6th century), Gubbio recovered and by the 11th century had become an independent city-state. Its power increased following a series of victorious wars fought against neighbouring city-states, often allied among each other, and against powerful Perugia itself. The defence of its independence, the increase in its population (which reached 50,000 inhabitants), the erection of numerous monuments and the development of the noble artistic and cultural traditions that still characterize the town today all testify to Gubbio's political, economic and artistic prestige. Subsequently, the town was ruled by various lords, including the Montefeltro, the Malatesta and the Della Rovere, and only after the 17th century was joined to the Papal States, to which it belonged until its annexation to the Kingdom of Italy. It should also be recalled that towards the end of the Second World War the town suffered appalling reprisals by the occupying German forces, who executed 40 citizens of Gubbio in the square which has since been re-named Piazza Quaranta Martiri (Piazza of the Forty Martyrs) in commemoration of them.

Today, Gubbio is a town of the greatest interest thanks to its monumental centre, its splendid buildings and its unaltered medieval appearance. It is also famous for its "Corsa dei Ceri" (Race of the Candles), a historic folklore event unique in its kind, which we will describe in more detail below. Many other significant events of an artistic and cultural character also take place in the town.

Gubbio is the birthplace of many famous Italians including Oderisi da Gubbio (mentioned by Dante in the "Divine Comedy") and Gattapone (an architect and builder of a number of fortresses). For centuries, too, the highly sophisticated art of ceramics has flourished in Gubbio, a tradition which is still kept alive today.

PALAZZO DEI CONSOLI

Symbol of Gubbio's medieval power, its unmistakeable outline dominates the town, towering impressively but at the same time gracefully, over the close-knit cluster of medieval houses beneath it, its entrance overlooking the beautiful Piazza della Signoria.

Because of its enormous foundations and structure, the Palazzo dei Consoli has been attributed to the 14th century Gubbio architect Gattapone, whose buildings were always charac-terized by massive, powerful features.

Probably, Angelo da Orvieto was also involved in its design, as suggested by the fact that his name is inscribed over its main entrance.

Shaped like a parallelepiped, the palazzo is set high on a terrace and supported on great buttresses of stone.

The façade is plain and unadorned apart from the entrance-door, reached up a fan-shaped flight of steps, and a row of upper windows.

Along the roof there is a series of hanging arches and an attractive line of battlements. The interior, which boasts a vast and magnificent entrance hall, houses the Civic Museum and Picture Gallery.

In the grand *Salone* (Hall), the assemblies of the Consuls were held. Today, the Hall contains archaelogical finds, cinerary urns, inscriptions, sarcophagi, the ribs of a mammoth found during excavations in the area nearby and a beautiful painting by Nelli depicting a Madonna and Child.

MUSEUM AND PICTURE GALLERY IN THE PALAZZO DEI CONSOLI

The most precious exhibit of the Museum in the Palazzo dei Consoli is the above-mentioned series of Eugubine Tablets. These consist of seven bronze plates with inscriptions describing ancient religious rites, regulations and customs. As already mentioned, the tablets constitute the one surviving document of the Umbrian language; the alphabet used is Etruscan and Latin. They are of crucial importance as archaeological evidence of a civilization which belongs to the origins of human history, not only from a linguistic but also from a cultural point of view, since they shed light on the life and customs of one of the most important Italic peoples.

Picture Gallery
Below: Palazzo dei Consoli - Entrance hall.

The *Picture Gallery* contains a number of paintings mainly belonging to the local school, but also including some works by Tuscan masters. Pieces of sculpture and furniture from different periods are also on display. The Loggia of the Palazzo dei Consoli affords marvellous panoramic views over the whole of the town and beyond.

Above left: 14th century Christ.
Above: Eugubine Tablets.
Below: Polyptych by Guido Palmerucci.
Next page: Detail of "The Madonna of the Pomegranate", perhaps by Pier Francesco Fiorentino - The piece of work can't be seen anymore inside the picture gallery because it was stolen in 1979.

MT. INGINO - SANT'UBALDO - RACE OF THE CANDLES

The annual Corsa dei Ceri (Race of the Candles) is one of the most famous festivals in the world, one of the most lively, fascinating and phantasmagorical of events. A religious and folklore festival, both sacred and profane in that it unites the pagan rites of spring with the cult of the town's patron saint, it is also the most heartfelt expression of the people of Gubbio. It is an exciting event, consisting in the wild and reckless race of the Candles through the streets of the town up to the church of Sant'Ubaldo on the summit of Mt. Ingino overlooking Gubbio: it is exciting for the "ceraioli" (the bearers of the Can-

dles), for the local population, and for the spectator who finds himself caught up in the event despite himself thanks to the enthusiasm and the fever of excitement among the spectators, the clamour of the drums, and the exhilarating contest of strength and skill. The origins of the festival almost certainly date back to 1154, when Gubbio, to express its gratitude to St. Ubaldo, the bishop of the town who had propitiated the victory of the city-state over an alliance of eleven neighbouring cities, decided to celebrate this historic event with an annual festival which would perpetuate the memory both of the victory and the Saint. In fact the Corsa dei Ceri merged and blended with a series of ancient local festivals that had been held for centuries: thanksgiving rites in honour of the spring and of nature, the bestower of life and prosperity.

It is invariably celebrated - and has been for centuries - on the 15th May. One interesting fact in this connection, testifying to the meaning this event holds for the people of Gubbio, is that in wartime, in the absence of male citizens, the Race was run by women instead.

The Candles consist of three huge wooden constructions, octagonal in shape and up to 7 metres in height. On the top of each Candle is the statue of a Saiant: St. Ubaldo, patron of the town and protector of masons, St. George, protector of merchants, and St. Anthony, protector of agricultural workers. The "ceraioli" who carry the Candles wear special costumes for the race, consisting of fez, scarf, trousers and shirt, each bearer wearing a different colour: yellow for St. Ubaldo, blue for St. George and black for St. Anthony. After a complex ceremony which has remained unaltered for centuries and recalls social figures and customs dating back to the Middle Ages, at 11 o'clock on the 15 May, the three Candles are raised onto the shoulders on their bearers and carried in procession through the streets of the town to Piazza della Signoria.

After being blessed by the bishop, in the afternoon the Mayor gives the signal for the race to begin: a race in which the Candles are carried at breakneck speed to the top of the hill, to the entrance of the church of Sant'Ubaldo. The climb is steep and the street narrow: during the race, because the Candles are so heavy, the bearers need to take turns. It is a reckless, sometimes dramatic, contest which only ends once the tomb of the Saint has been reached and the Candles have been placed on it, while the bearers, to complete the rite, beat the wooden constructions loudly with their hands. The winner

is established in a somewhat unusual way: it is not the first to arrive that wins, because the order in which the Candles set off at the starting point does not and cannot change along the route.

The order is always the same each year: first St. Ubaldo, second St. George, and third St. Anthony. The winner is decided on the basis of the skill shown during the race: dropping the Candle, for example, is considered a disgrace for the team to which it belongs, while it is a source of honour for the first or second Candle to increase the distance between itself and the one behind, so as to reach the doorway of Sant'Ubaldo and close it before the arrival of the other team or, by the same token, for the second or third Candle to close the gap between itself and the one in front and rest the poles of their Candle on it. The greater or lesser degree of skill shown by each of the three teams in running the race is discussed endlessly by the people of Gubbio for days after the event.

Another interesting feature of Gubbio is the tallest *Christmas tree* in the world, made in 1981 by a group of churchgoers from Sant'Ubaldo. Situated on Mt. Ingino, where the Basilica of Sant'Ubaldo stands, it is 350 metres high, is made up of 12 kilometres of electrical cables and is lit up by 450 light-bulbs.

Twice a year a *Crossbow Tournament* (Palio della Balestra) is held in costume; in May it is held in Piazza della Signoria in Gubbio and in September in the town of San Sepolcro. The target for the competitors to hit is hung on Palazzo Pretorio, and the winner is awarded a banner (the palio) as his prize. During the tournament there are performances of flag-waving. Another crossbow tournament is held among the different districts of the town. An interesting itinerary for the visitor is a tour of the North Umbria towns of *Scheggia, Sigillo, Gualdo Tadino* (renowned for its artistic ceramics factories and its medieval monuments) and *Nocera Umbra*, whose name is associated with springs of mineral water.

Some phases of the race of the wax candles.

Right: The tallest tree in the world. Below: The Crossbow Tournament.

ASSISI

A precious medieval jewel, set against a lovely natural backdrop, Assisi can be considered, more than any other Umbrian town, as the symbol of the religious and mystical soul of the region.

It was here that St. Francis was born and founded his new religious order; it was here too that St. Clare lived and worked. The whole town is permeated with Franciscan memories and its most significant monuments are those built to commemorate its saints. Famous artists, first and foremost Giotto, have embellished its churches.

A gentle, quiet and intimate atmosphere reigns in the town. To this is added the unforgettable impression made by its medieval appearance, its charming surrounding landscape, its houses built out of the pink stone of Subasio.

Originally an Umbrian town, it was conquered by the Romans and rose to considerable importance during Roman times, as testified by remains still visible in the town. Devastated during the barbarian invasions, Assisi later became a free city-state and fought to defend its independence, especially against the neighbouring town of Perugia (the young St. Francis took part in these struggles). After the death of the Saint in 1226, the town was embellished with magnificent churches and great pictorial masterpieces like those of Giotto.

During the Renaissance Assisi was ruled by various lords before becoming part of the Papal States. Today the town has become one of the main tourist centres not only of Umbria but of the whole of Italy. There are two main reasons for this: firstly, its attractions in the architectural and artistic field, represented in particular by the Basilica of Saint Francis and secondly and just as important, its significance for Christians as a result of the many religious

and cultural events linked to the commemoration of the town's great Saints, Francis and Clare.

BASILICA OF SAN FRANCESCO (ST. FRANCIS'S)

The vision that awaits those who enter the lower part of Piazza San Francesco is unforgettable: at the far end of the square rises the façade of the church, with its simple, harmonious, graceful lines, while a low, unadorned colonnade runs along the sides, which at one time provided shelter for the pilgrims and the sick who came to visit the tomb of the Saint.

Quietness, tranquillity, a contemplative and mystical atmosphere: everything seems to be pervaded with the spirit of St. Francis.

At the far end of the square, next to the *Oratory of San Bernardino* and the entrance to the *Monastery*, is the elegant doorway of the Lower Church. Distinguished by the huge round arch in which it is set, it consists of a composite but well-balanced series of gothic arches enclosing a double door.

The elegance and beauty of this façade are enriched by the subtle interplay of coloured marble and mosaic decoration.

The Basilica is a grandiose and impressive temple built in honour of the Poverello (Poor Man) of Assisi, and captures the visitor's attention even before he has entered the town: the huge complex can in fact be seen from a distance, rising majestically over the enormous mass of its foundations and great blind arches supported by the terraces of the hillside.

The building of the Basilica was begun immediately after the death of St. Francis at the wish of Brother Elias, his successor as head of the order of the Friars Minor, and also thanks to the personal interest shown by Pope Gregory IX.

Brother Elias also designed the church, though other architects were also involved, especially after his death.

The Basilica consists of two superimposed churches (plus a third constituted by the Crypt in which the Saint's body lies), facing in different directions to avoid subsidence or landslides.

A large part of the building was

already completed by 1230, the year in which St. Francis's remains were solemnly laid to rest in it. The whole complex was virtually completed by 1253, at least as regards its structure; its pictorial decoration was to be added later.

ST. FRANCIS

It is impossible to talk about Assisi without talking about St. Francis, a man who is dear to the hearts of so many people irrespective of their religious beliefs.

Patron saint of Italy and also of ecology, he was born to a wealthy family of merchants in Assisi in 1182. His youth was spent in a lively, carefree fashion. Like many other young men, he fought in the war against the neighbouring town of Perugia.

Following an illness which confined him to bed for a long time, he began a life of meditation. From there it was but a short step to the conversion which was soon to lead to a decisive turning-point in his life.

Divesting himself publicly of his fine clothes in front of his parents, the Bishop and the townspeople, he began a life of absolute poverty and penance.

Soon followed by other young people, including Saint Clare, he laid down a series of principles to which his community was expected to conform; these were Poverty, Chastity and Obedience. Francis sought official papal approval of the order he had founded, which he obtained in two steps: first he obtained formal approval by Pope Innocent III; and second, official ratification of his Rule and the Order of the Friars Minor by Honorius III in 1223. Francis travelled extensively to propagate the teaching of Christ and above all to restore Christianity to its original essence: purity, humility, forgiveness, simplicity, love for all God's creatures. He died on the 3rd October 1226 at the Portiuncula, the place where he had established his first community and his Rule.

Two years previously the Saint had received the Stigmata on Mt. La Verna; he died, as he had lived, poor and humble.

In 1230 his body was transferred to the Basilica of San Francesco, which in the meantime had been erected to perpetuate his memory and to honour his remains.

ST. CLARE

St. Clare was born in a wealthy family in Assisi in 1193 or 1194. Although she received a thorough religious education, it was the fervent and passionate preaching of her contemporary, St. Francis, that brought about the fundamental choices in her life.

She followed his example and embraced his Rule which was also accepted by her mother and sister and other women of Assisi. She founded the Order of the Clarisses (or Poor Clares), initially called the "Poor Ladies".

She died in 1253.

Basilica of San Francesco.

LOWER CHURCH OF SAN FRANCESCO

The wonderful interior is filled with meditative silence and a serene religious atmosphere. The pictorial decorations are of breathtaking beauty and the shadowy half-light that permeates the whole church, together with an unusual architectural structure distinguished by broad, low gothic vaulting, creates a singular effect. The church is in the form of a Latin cross, preceded by a wing which recalls the antechamber or narthex of Early Christian churches. The sculptures and paintings which embellish the interior are of the greatest interest; we will mention only the most important of them here, though it should be said that the frescoes as a whole are of the highest artistic value.

The wonderful Chapel of St. Martin, completely frescoed by Simone Martini with scenes from the life of St. Martin, is one of the most beautiful works of the painter and a masterpiece of Gothic art. In the transept of the church there is a cycle of frescoes, unfortunately damaged, attributable to great artists like Pietro Lorenzetti (the "Crucifixion", a "Madonna and Child" and a "Deposition"), Giotto himself and some of his followers.

There are also frescoes by Cimabue (a "Madonna and Child"), by the so-called Maestro of St. Francis and by the Maestro of the Assisi Vaults, so named because he decorated the vaulting above the high altar with the "Allegories of Poverty, Chastity and Obedience" and "The Apotheosis of St. Francis".

In the Chapel of the Relics (Cappella delle Reliquie), St. Francis's belongings are kept: his tunic, the sandals he rarely wore and the piece of cloth with which he wiped the blood from his Stigmata.

Lower church - "Enthroned Virgin with Angels and St. Francis" - Cimabue (ca. 1280).

Lower Church - Interior.

Below: Lower Church - "Madonna of te Sunset", (Pietro Lorenzetti).

THE CRYPT

The entrance to the crypt is located halfway down the nave of the lower church; a stairway leads down to it. It is here that the mortal remains of St. Francis are preserved.

The Saint's body was transferred here in 1230 by the same Brother Elias who commissioned the building of the Basilica; hitherto the Saint had been temporarily interred in the church of San Giorgio (now annexed to the church of Santa Chiara). The simple stone tomb of the Saint stands at the centre of the chamber behind a wrought-iron grate, which is protected in turn by a tabernacle of recent construction, against which an altar stands. The tombs of some of St. Francis's closest companions are placed round the walls of the crypt: Leone, Rufino, Matteo and Angelo.

In the middle of the crypt hangs the votive lamp which each year, on the anniversary of the Saint's death, is filled with oil offered in turn by the various towns and regions of Italy.

Originally the crypt was far more simple and rudimentary in structure; today it is adorned by the great tabernacle over the tomb and its walls are entirely covered with a lining of marble.

In spite of these transformations and embellishments, the crypt remains a place of silence and meditation, pervaded by the profoundly mystic and moving atmosphere inspired by the presence of the Saint's tomb.

Lower Church - Chapel of the Magdalena.

Lower Church - Crypt, the tomb with the sarcophagus in which the remains of St. Francis are preserved.

INTERIOR OF THE UPPER CHURCH: GIOTTO'S FRESCOES

Giotto's frescoes in the upper church constitute one of the most important cycles of painting in the history of Italian art.

The walls of the single nave were frescoed completely by Giotto who, in 28 scenes, depicts the salient episodes of the life of St. Francis, taken from the early biography of the Saint, the "Legenda Major" by St. Buonaventura.

The frescoes are unforgettable masterpieces: Giotto's figures impose themselves on our attention with the solidity of their forms and the eloquence of their gestures; the story unfolds in the pictures with great simplicity, clarity and power of expression; the solidity of the figures and landscapes creates, for the first time, a sense of perspective and a three-dimensional quality. But, most of all, the hand of the great artist has succeeded in giving a human, albeit epic and grandiose, dimension to the life of St. Francis and this enhances both the figure of the Saint and the art of Giotto.

The individual scenes are as follows (starting from the right wall after the altar):

1) *The offer of a cloak to St. Francis;*
2) *St. Francis gives his cloak to a poor man;*
3) *St. Francis has a vision of the weapons destined for the Crusade;*
4) *The crucifix urges St. Francis to restore its church (San Damiano);*
5) *St. Francis divests himself of his clothes;*
6) *Pope Innocent III has a vision of St. Francis supporting his Church;*
7) *Innocent III approves the Rule;*
8) *Vision of a chariot of fire;*
9) *St. Francis's appointed seat in heaven;*
10) *St. Francis drives the evil spirits from Arezzo;*
11) *St. Francis challenges the Muslims;*
12) *St. Francis in ecstasy;*
13) *St. Francis sets up the crib at Greccio;*
14) *St. Francis miraculously produces a spring of water;*
15) *St. Francis preaching to the birds;*
16) *Death of the lord of Celan;*
17) *St. Francis before Pope Honorius III;*
18) *St. Francis appears to the Friars of Arles;*
19) *St. Francis receives the Stigmata;*
20) *Death of St. Francis;*
21) *St. Francis appears to the Bishop of Assisi;*
22) *Jerome is convinced by the Stigmata of St. Francis;*
23) *The Saint's body is transferred;*
24) *Canonization;*
25) *St. Francis appears to Gregory IX;*
26) *St. Francis cures a wounded man;*
27) *St. Francis resuscitates a dead person;*
28) *St. Francis frees Pietro di Alife.*

Basilica of San Francesco - Cloister of Sixtus IV (15th century) and apse.

Basilica of San Francesco - the colonnade (13th century); in the background, the Umbrian plain and the stream Tescio.

Upper Church: The Vault with the Doctors of the Church by Giotto, damaged by the earthquake of 26th September 1997.

Upper Church: The vault of the Crossing, with the four Evangelists and Christ, demaged by the earthquake of 26th September 1997.

The young Francis is honoured by the simpleton of the town.

St. Francis prays before the crucifix of San Damino.

The dream of arms.

The Saint gives his cloak to a poor knight.

The death of St. Francis.
Below: The appearance at the Chapter-meeting at Arles.
Next page: The expulsion of the demons from Arezzo.

PIAZZA DEL COMUNE

Piazza del Comune is the political and administrative centre of Assisi and is also the site of its origins as here stood the Forum of the Roman town Asisium, still visible underneath the ground in the square. A splendid heritage from Roman times is the *Temple of Minerva*; the original appearance of the exterior has been well preserved, but the interior was transformed in the 16th and 17th centuries into the church of Santa Maria sopra Minerva and has therefore taken on Baroque forms. The temple is a beautiful testimony of Roman art and proves the importance of Assisi in Roman times. It was built at the end of the 1st century B.C. or at the very beginning of the 1st century A.D. The front of the temple consists of 6 handsome fluted columns, each resting on a pedestal, with Corinthian capitals, and a rather low, prominent pediment. Steps between the columns used to lead down to the Forum in Roman times. Inside, the old walls of the temple are visible, supporting beams and divided up by pilaster strips ending in Corinthian capitals.

In the square is a 14th century *pulpit* used in the past by San Bernardino da Siena for preaching and a *niche* with the remains of a fresco painted by the school of Simone Martini. The *Palazzo del Capitano del Popolo*, with its high and imposing crenellated tower is an impressive building. Built originally in the 13th century, it was later enlarged and altered. The handsome *Tower* standing next to it also dates from the 13th century; it has two orders of large arches and is crenellated with Ghibelline battlements.

On the southern side of the square is the *Palazzo dei Priori*, which in fact consists of several buildings of simple and austere appearance. Of particular interest is the *Volta Pinta* (Painted Vault), one of the large arches on the façade of the building which has been decorated with grotesques in a decidedly original manner.

The Palazzo dei Priori houses the *Pinacoteca* (Picture Gallery), a valuable collection of objects of varied origin and sculptures and paintings by different artists and of different eras.

Temple of Minerva and Civic Tower.

CATHEDRAL OF SAN RUFINO

Dedicated to St. Rufino, Bishop of Assisi in the 3rd century A.D., the Cathedral is one of the finest and most distinctive examples of Romanesque architecture in Umbria. The original church was completely altered and rebuilt in the 12th century and completed in the 13th century. An inscription inside the church attributes its design to Giovanni da Gubbio.

The Romanesque façade is particularly beautiful. The lower part is divided into rectangular compartments, above which is an elegant gallery. In the upper part there are three large rose-windows. Three handsome doorways, all with graceful carving around them, lead into the church.

The interior of the Cathedral has, by contrast, almost entirely lost its original appearance and in fact was redesigned by Galeazzo Alessi in the 16th century. Notable works of art to be seen in the Cathedral include Dono Doni's "Crucifixion" and "Deposition", a particularly expressive "Pietà" of German workmanship, fine 16th-century wooden choir-stalls and the Baptismal Font (carved from a monolithic block of granite) in which Saint Francis and Saint Clare were baptized.

Of particular interest is the Crypt (11th century) which still retains its suggestive Romanesque structure. It is also worth visiting the Cathedral Museum (Museo Capitolare) which contains objects from the original church of San Rufino.

SANTA CHIARA (ST. CLARE'S)

St. Clare, follower of St. Francis and founder of the Order of the Poor Clares, just as gentle and serene a figure as her contemporary St Francis, lies buried in the crypt of this church dedicated to her. In its architectural style, the church resembles the upper basilica of San Francesco, differing from it in its greater simplicity and more modest decoration.

Along the left side of the church, massive arches rest on the building. The façade is characterized by horizontal bands of marble of contrasting colours and a rose-window.

The interior contains a large altarpiece depicting the most significant episodes from the life of the Saint, attributed to the so-called Maestro of St. Clare. The church also houses the Crucifix which, according to tradition, spoke to St. Francis urging him to rebuild the church in which it was kept at the time: the small church of San Damiano.

A number of relics of St. Clare are displayed in the church and her mortal remains lie in the crypt below.

The Crucifix which spoke to St. Francis in 1206 in the church of San Damiano (12th century).

CHURCH OF SAN DAMIANO

This solitary church on the outskirts of Assisi provides us with a more profound and direct contact with the Franciscan spirit.

It was here that St. Francis probably wrote his famous canticle to the sun and moon, and here that he heard the voice of Christ urging him to restore the church which in fact lay in ruins at the time. It was here, too, that he gathered with the first of his followers and that Saint Clare also stayed. The little church, situated in a secluded site in the peaceful Umbrian countryside, is extremely simple and plain.

In front of it there is a low portico and there are side chapels with 16th century frescoes. The interior, just as simple as the exterior, has a single nave, notably prolonged towards the apse, whose shape is reminiscent of a deep cave. The atmosphere of the church as a whole is extremely suggestive: the mysterious half-light, the rough, dark walls, the few frescoes recording one of the Saint's miracles, the Franciscan spirit with which every corner is permeated, the cloister and the little rooms in which Saint Clare lived, everything makes a profound impression on us and gives us a better understanding of the Franciscan spirit.

FESTIVITIES AND TRADITIONS

The May-Day festivity called the *Calendimaggio* (calendae being a Roman term to indicate the first day of the month) takes place between the last day of April and the first day of May and is of pagan origin though the people of Assisi have, over the years, tried to commemorate Francis and recall his carefree youth on this occasion.

It is an outburst of joy and purity, of songs and music, of traditional costumes and flowers. It is the celebration and exaltation of Spring expressed in people and things with the joy of life.

This festival is felt strongly by the people of Assisi who take part in it wearing faithfully reproduced historical costumes. The focal point of the festival is a contest between the two districts (the lower district and the higher district) into which Assisi is divided, and the aim is to win the "palio" (a finely decorated banner).

The judges award the banner to the district with the better costumes, songs, flagwaving skills, and results in the cross-bow competitions.

Among the religious events that take place in Assisi, we would mention the *Pardon of Assisi*, which commemorates the indulgence obtained by St. Francis (on the occasion of the official approval of his Rule from Pope Honorius III), for all those who go to the Portiuncula asking forgiveness for their sins.

It takes place from July 31 to August 2, drawing crowds of pilgrims from all over the world.

Other religious festivities take place to commemorate the death of St. Francis (4 October) and that of St. Clare (12 August). Other festivities are connected with the major events on the Church calendar such as *Holy Week*, Ascension Day, Pentecost, Corpus Domini.

Particularly interesting and suggestive are the ceremonies which take place during Holy Week, including processions along the streets of the town with hooded friars bearing crosses and the symbols of Christ's Passion,

and other monks and people bearing torches, and a live enactment of the "Deposition from the Cross", after the manner of historical religious plays.

We would also mention the processions and the rites celebrated on certain days of the month (on Fridays and Sundays) and which usually take place after sunset, when the Franciscan Friars congregate in the Basilica of San Francesco and in the square in front of it in order to commemorate the Saint and some of the episodes in his life.

Although these ceremonies and events are mainly religious in character, almost all of them contain historical or traditional elements (processions in costume and ancient rites that have been passed down through the centuries) that add a special charm to them.

HERMITAGE
(EREMO DELLE CARCERI)

This is the name given to the small monastery which stands on the spot where St. Francis was fond of retiring in solitude to pray.

In the Umbrian countryside there are many spots like this. In fact, it was a habit of St. Francis to find shelter in wild inaccessible spots, in direct contact with nature. The bare ground was his bed, wild fruit his food, caves his only shelter. It is just this extreme humility, this total and seraphic acceptance of the Christian spirit, which exalts his true stature. Moreover, it is just in hermitages like this that the spirit that animated the Franciscan movement can be most deeply felt.

The Monastery was gradually built after St. Francis's death by those of his companions and followers who, like their Master, withdrew to the spot to meditate and do penance. The first cells and refectory were hollowed out of the rock around an existing chapel dedicated to Santa Maria delle Carceri (Holy Lady of Prisons).

All the rooms in the monastery are characterized by their extreme austerity and cramped space. Particularly moving is the bed of rock St. Francis slept on; it leaves one almost incredulous. But the whole hermitage is pervaded with an intense and suggestive atmosphere of peace and serenity, an invitation to silence, meditation and prayer.

The woodland that extends round the Hermitage on the slopes of Monte Subasio is also worth a visit, both for its associations with St. Francis and for its unspoiled beauty.

BASILICA OF SANTA MARIA DEGLI ANGELI

The Basilica of Santa Maria degli Angeli is situated at the foot of the hill on which Assisi stands. Its proud outline, its splendid white marble and the gilded statue placed on top of its façade which glitters in the sun, all stand out clearly in the plain beneath the town of Assisi.

The Basilica was built to provide a suitably monumental setting for some of the most hallowed spots associated with the life of Saint Francis: the Portiuncula (the simple hut in which the Saint gathered with his followers when he began preaching and drew up the guidelines for his Order), the Chapel of Transit (Cappella del Transito), built over the spot where he died, and the Chapel of Roses (Cappella delle Rose), another spot beloved by the Saint. The Basilica was designed by Galeazzo Alessi in the 16th century, but was almost completely rebuilt by Luigi Poletti in the 19th century and by Bazzani in the 20th century, after the church had been seriously damaged by an earthquake.

The façade is built in an imitation Renaissance style intermixed with baroque features.

The interior, grandiose in its vast proportions, has a basilica-type plan with a series of richly decorated side chapels.

PORTIUNCULA

When St. Francis chose it as his dwelling it was a tiny Benedictine chapel which had probably been built in the 9th century.

It was a simple, secluded place, surrounded by fields and woodland; later, when the number of the Saint's followers increased, it was restored and little huts were built around it for the friars. It was here that St. Francis drew up the Rule which was to be the foundation of the Order of the Friars Minor and which was based on the three principles of Poverty, Obedience and Chastity, symbolized by the three knots in the cord that the Franciscans wear around their habits. Now situated under the dome of the Basilica of Santa Maria degli Angeli, the chapel has a gothic façade, while its extremely plain, humble and unadorned interior is moving because it so perfectly embodies the spirit of poverty pursued by St. Francis. The chapel is now linked with the indulgence of the Perdono, or Pardon of St. Francis.

It is here that the feast of the Perdono is celebrated in early August each year, attracting vast throngs of pilgrims from all over Italy.

Chapel of the Portiuncula.

Basilica of Santa Maria degli Angeli.

CHAPEL OF TRANSIT (CAPPELLA DEL TRANSITO)

Transformed into a chapel immediately after the death of St. Francis and subsequently embellished, it was at one time used as an infirmary, a place where the sick could be treated, as the Saint had wished.

And it was here, lying on the bare ground as was his habit, that the Saint, serene to the end, welcomed what he loved to call "our sister - bodily death".

The Chapel contains some frescoes and a fine glazed terracotta statue of the Saint by Andrea Della Robbia.

ROSE GARDEN

This small garden is famous for its beautiful thornless roses. According to religious tradition, St. Francis, to escape the Devil's temptations, threw himself naked into them and the roses, as a sign of contrition for having torn his body, lost their thorns, while their leaves were marked with his blood.

It is still possible, in fact, to distinguish the red flecks with which the leaves are marked.

On one side of the garden stands the beautiful Chapel of the Roses (Cappella delle Rose); it consists of three different parts (including the cave in which St. Francis used to pray) and is decorated with frescoes of the life of the Saint by Tiberio d'Assisi (1518).

MUSEUM

To visit the Museum one must be accompanied by a monk.

In the first room are kept precious sacred vestments, relics and reliquaries. In the two succeeding rooms, among many paintings, there are three of very great value: the Crucifixion by Giunta Pisano, of 1236; Saint Francis between two Angels, by the «Master of Saint Francis», (in the book the Saint holds in his hands is written: "This tablet was my repose in life and in death"; the portrait of Saint Francis attributed to Cimabue (after the cleaning of the fresco of Cimabue in the Lower Church of the Basilica of Saint Francis, a great resemblance was noted between the two portraits).

SPELLO

Spello is one of the most characteristically Umbrian towns. Picturesquely situated on the slopes of one of the foothills of Mt. Subasio, it is also one of the most interesting towns on account of its Roman remains, its delightful medieval appearance and its Renaissance monuments. Spello was called Hispellum in Roman times and grew to such considerable importance as to be called "colonia splendidissima Julia". In the Middle Ages, it first came under the Duchy of Spoleto and then the Papal States, before passing under the domination of neighbouring Perugia. It was later ruled by various lords, before returning under the control of the Papal States in the 16th century.

A visit to Spello should include a stroll through the old town centre, in which the most typical and picturesque features of medieval Umbria are to be seen. In addition to the monuments described below, the following churches are worth visiting: the Romanesque church of Sant'Andrea, with frescoes by Pinturicchio; the church of San Lorenzo with a number of fine paintings and sculptures; the church of San Claudio (on the outskirts), small but of interest due to its unusual design based on distorted proportions, aimed at producing peculiar optical effects; and lastly the church known as the Chiesa Tonda (Round Church), dating from the 16th century.

Overlooking the town above is the Rocca (Fortress), which dates back to the 14th century but is now reduced to little more than a tower. Close by is the small church of the Cappuccini and the splendid Belvedere, from which panoramic views can be enjoyed.

We can end our visit by wandering through the town's streets and squares, imagining without much difficulty how life must have been in the past, continuing as it does here into the present.

FOLIGNO

Moving southwards from Spello, the Umbrian Valley broadens out into an ample plain watered by the River Topino.

Here Foligno is situated, a large modern industrial town, of interest for its historic centre and a number of noteworthy monuments and works of art. Originally an Umbrian settlement, it was conquered by the Romans and was given the name of Fulginiae. The layout of the town, based on the typical Roman street plan, dates back to this period.

At the time of the barbarian invasions, it was devastated a number of times like so many other Umbrian towns. But in the period of the medieval city-states it became a political, social and cultural centre of increasing importance.

The height of its fortune came in the 14th and 15th centuries when it was ruled by the Trinci family, which succeeded in extending its territory well beyond the town limits, annexing towns further afield like Montefalco, Spello and Assisi.

In the 15th century, it was also renowned for the beginning of the art of printing in Italy: it was in Foligno that the first printed editions of important works such as Dante's Divine Comedy appeared. After the fall of the Trinci, Foligno was annexed to the Papal States.

Many attractions make a visit to Foligno of particular interest: its buildings and churches, which testify eloquently to the vitality of its artistic and cultural life and also the traditional festivities which take place there each year, the major one being the Quintana Jousting Tournament.

PIAZZA DELLA REPUBBLICA

The central point of Foligno, Piazza della Repubblica also contains some of the town's finest and most interesting buildings, such as the Cathedral, the Palazzo Comunale and the Palazzo Trinci.

The *Cathedral* (Duomo), built at the beginning of the 12th century and then altered and enlarged later, has two façades, one looking onto Piazza del Duomo and the other onto Piazza della Repubblica. The latter, Romanesque in style, is particularly handsome, with a fine doorway, above which there is a series of arch-es between two elegant rose-win-dows. The interior has been redesigned several times, by Pier-marini and Vanvitelli among others. The crypt is built out of material from an earlier church. In the presbytery there is a fine statue of St. Feliciano, patron saint of Foligno, by G.B. Maini.

The 14th century *Palazzo Trinci* houses the *Picture Gallery* and con-tains numerous rooms frescoed by Ottaviano Nelli, Mezzastris, Bar-tolomeo di Tommaso and Benozzo Gozzoli.

Other buildings worth a visit include the Romanesque *church of Santa Maria Infraportas*, built in the 11th century and containing frescoes and paintings in the Byzantine style, the 13th century *church of San Salvatore* with fine Gothic doorways and poly-chrome decorations, and the church-es of the *Nunziatella*, of *San Giaco-mo* and *San Nicolò*.

Near Foligno, situated in a glorious natural setting, is the *Abbey of Sasso-vivo (Abbazia di Sassovivo)*, built by Benedictine monks in the 11th centu-ry. The Romanesque cloister, designed by Pietro di Maria in the 13th century and consisting in an ele-gant portico with paired columns, is of great charm.

Piazza della Repubblica.

QUINTANA JOUSTING TOURNAMENT (GIOSTRA DELLA QUINTANA)

The Quintana Tournament is an annual event which recalls the costumes, festivities and contests on horseback of the past. It dates back at least to the 17th century, but was probably already being celebrated, in a different form, at an even earlier date. The Tournament takes place in the town stadium in mid-September. It consists of a contest in which ten riders, one for each district of the town, attempt to thread their lance through a ring hanging from a puppet while galloping on horseback. The contest itself is preceded by a series of traditional ceremonies and by a splendid historical procession in period costumes which, in the early afternoon, winds its way through the streets of the town, bearing the Gonfalone (the town banner) and coats of arms of the various districts. The Tournament is a memorable event, not only for the splendour of its costumes and the skill and competitive spirit shown in the horseback contest, but also for the special atmosphere which any event aimed at recalling historical traditions succeeds in creating.

BEVAGNA

Known as Mevania in Roman times, when it was a flourishing municipium, Bevagna still preserves traces of its Roman origins. But it was in the Middle Ages that the town acquired its most important buildings, especially those around Piazza Silvestri, the heart of the old centre. The visitor should note the 13th century *Palazzo dei Consoli*, with its large arches and wide flight of steps at its side, which houses the Tortiti Theatre, and the lovely *church of San Silvestro*, a masterpiece of architecture designed by Binello in 1195 with a simple, graceful façade.

The 13th century *Cathedral*, dedicated to St. Michael, is a fine example of Romanesque architecture with its elegant doorway and horizontal line of arches which distinguish the façade.

MONTEFALCO

Montefalco is one of Umbria's most delightful towns, thanks to its charming position (it is called the balustrade of Umbria) and its artistic treasures, considered among the most important works of art not only in Umbria but in the whole of Italy.

Its greatest treasures are the splendid paintings and frescoes to be found in its churches, especially those left by Benozzo Gozzoli. The decoration of the churches and town buildings of Montefalco in the 14th and 15th centuries was favoured by the patronage of the Papal Rectors

who resided there.

The *church of San Francesco* was built in the 14th century and transformed in the 16th century. It acts as a picture gallery and houses works not only by Gozzoli (the series of frescoes depicting the life of St. Francis, painted around the middle of the 15th century, and those portraying St. Jerome are breathtakingly beautiful) but also by Mezzastris, Melanzio and Alunno.

The *church of Sant'Agostino*, built between the 13th and 14th centuries, houses a precious cycle of frescoes, a splendid example of 14th and 15th century Umbrian painting.

Other noteworthy paintings by the Umbrian school are to be found in the *church of Santa Chiara*, with its lovely chapel of the Holy Cross, and in the splendid *church of Santa Illuminata*.

Above: Bevagna - Church of St. Michael.
Below: Montefalco - Piazza del Comune.

TREVI

The town of Trevi is a wonderful sight from a distance, clearly silhouetted against the sky, its white houses clinging to the top of a hill and the peaks of Mt. Serano and Mt. Brunette rising behind it.

In Roman times it was known as Trebiae, but the Roman town was not situated on top of the hill, like its modern counterpart, but on the valley floor near the important Via Flaminia.

Today, Trevi is a town of great interest on account of its monuments and its typical medieval appearance and atmosphere.

A visit to Trevi should take in its churches: the 14th century *San Martino*, which contains works by Mezzastris and Tiberio d'Assisi; *San Francesco*, in the Gothic style; and *Sant'Emiliano*, originally built in 1100, but altered in later centuries. Parts of its original structure, for example the apse, may still be admired, and the church also contains a graceful 16th century altar. Also worth visiting at Trevi is the interesting municipal *Picture Gallery* housed in a suite of rooms in the *Palazzo Comunale*.

The works on display include a fine "Madonna and Child with Angels and St. Francis" by Spagna and another "Madonna and Child" by Pinturicchio. A number of interesting excursions may be made in the area around Trevi. Just outside the town is the *church of the Madonna delle Lacrime*, built in the Renaissance style in the 15th century. The church contains paintings by both Spagna and Perugino, but many other works of art by other Umbrian artists are also worth noticing.

The church acquired its name - Madonna of Tears - because tradition narrates that the picture of the Madonna over the high altar was once seen to weep.

Equally worth visiting is the *church of Santa Maria di Pietrarossa*, which is decorated with frescoes of various periods, mainly by local artists.

The sources of the Clitumnus (Le Fonti del Clitunno)

"Hail, verdant Umbria, and you of the pure spring, deified Clitumnus!"

It is in these words from a famous ode that the Italian poet Giosué Carducci described this spot that so many writers of antiquity had already praised and admired before him.

The sources of the Clitumnus: an enchanting and unique spot, an oasis of exceptional beauty and peace, a scenario of colour and light, a marvellous blend of so many natural elements.

The lush vegetation, mainly poplars and weeping willows, is reflected in the crystal-clear waters of the little lake. Here the intense colours create exceptional reflections and everything seems to hover on the borders of the fairy-tale and the unreal. Not unnaturally, the ancients, enchanted by this idyllic scene, supposed that the god Clitumnus, a river god who dispensed his oracles from the depths of the waters, resided here. It was here, too, that the Romans believed that sacrificial animals should be brought for purification, because they believed that only this lake, with the purity and limpidity of its waters, had the power to make them pure and spotless.

In reality, the spring of the Clitumnus, transparent and charming though it may be, is simply overflowing water which wells up from the depths of the rock below.

The *Roman Temple of the Clitumnus* is situated close by, a small, harmonious building later converted into an Early Christian church dedicated to San Salvatore.

SPOLETO

Spoleto, the town of the Festival of the Two Worlds, which attracts tourists from all over the world every year with its cultural events of the highest standard, is magnificently situated over gently-sloping hills, dominated by its proud castle and the densely-wooded slopes of Monteluco behind it.

More richly endowed with historic monuments, especially of the medieval period, than most other cities in Umbria or even in Italy, Spoleto is an unforgettable town for its beauty and for being the centre of an arts festival of international stature, as well as the venue of important study conferences, such as the annual Congress on the Early Middle Ages. Spoleto's history is a distinguished one. Founded in prehistoric times, it was occupied by the ancient Umbrians, under whom it rose to political power and economic importance.

It later became a flourishing and splendid Roman town with the name of Spoletium (a name of Etruscan origin, suggesting a temporary ascendancy of Etruscan civilization over part of this territory).

After suffering under the Gothic invasions, Spoleto was occupied by the Lombards and, in the 6th century, became the capital of the Duchy of Spoleto which rapidly rose to such great political importance that its dukes aspired to the imperial crown itself.

It was during the same period that the town extended its rule over the surrounding territory until a large part of Central Italy lay under its control. Weakened by the major defeat inflicted on it by Frederick Barbarossa, Spoleto came under the control of the Papal States from the 12th century onwards. In the ensuing period it was torn by continuous civil strife and was characterized by alternating periods of greater or lesser splendour and importance. Essentially, however, its history was not dissimilar from that of many other Umbrian towns, though it maintained a pre-eminent historical and cultural role.

CATHEDRAL (DUOMO)

A masterpiece of architecture, the splendid Cathedral of Santa Maria Assunta is a combination of various styles and materials which testify to the various stages of its construction, blended together in a harmonious whole. The building even incorporates materials dating from the Roman period, visible in the bell-tower. The main structure of the church is, however, medieval, as is obvious from its façade, although the elegant portico in front of the Cathedral dates from the Renaissance.

The building is situated at the far end of Piazza del Duomo and forms the backdrop to the gala concert with which the town's Arts Festival comes to a close each year.

The façade is particularly interesting: it is divided into three vertical sections by pilaster strips, decorated by slightly pointed arches and a number of rose-windows. At its centre, a richly decorated doorway leads into the nave of the church. Above, a large mosaic of Christ occupies the central arch of the upper storey.

The interior of the Cathedral contains a series of splendid works of art. Particularly worthy of note are the frescoes by Filippo Lippi in the apse, a masterpiece of Renaissance art. Paintings by Pinturicchio, a statue of Pope Urban VIII by Bernini and a fine Byzantine icon venerated in the Chapel of the Holy Icon should also be noted. In the right transept is the tomb of Filippo Lippi, the Florentine artist who decorated the apse of the church and who died before he could finish his frescoes. A number of important documents and an autograph of St. Francis of Assisi are preserved in the adjoining presbytery.

Cathedral of Santa Maria Assunta - Coronation of the Virgin (Filippo Lippi).

ROMAN THEATRE

Dating from the 1st century A.D., the theatre remained buried under the ground for centuries and moreover was hidden by other buildings which were erected around it, but it has now been excavated completely and restored so that its original structure is once more visible.

CHURCH OF SAN PIETRO (ST. PETER'S)

This church is one of the finest and most important examples of Umbrian architecture. A masterpiece of Romanesque architecture, it stands out in particular for the superb bas-reliefs which decorate the façade, dating from the 12th and 13th centuries. The bas-reliefs depict sacred themes, often with symbolic figures, and are representative of an exquisite taste for decoration and incomparable sharpness and clarity of style. The church was built in the Middle Ages over a 5th century temple; in the 14th century it was restored and its structure was altered, but the splendid façade was left intact.

The *church of San Silvestro* is to be found nearby; built in the 13th century, it houses archaeological fragments of the Roman and early Christian period.

MONTELUCO

Behind Spoleto stands the hill of Monteluco, offering delightful scenic walks through the dense woods of holm oak that grow on its slopes right up to the summit. The wood has been considered sacred for thousands of years: as far back as pagan times it was used as a place of worship to the gods and later, with the spread of Christianity, it came to be inhabited by hermits who preferred to live in isolated spots in order to meditate and pray and remain in closer contact with nature. St. Francis, too, visited Monteluco and

Above: Roman theatre.
Below: Church of San Pietro.

90

founded a convent there, founded a convent there, which like all the places he lived in was simple and peaceful.

Several hermitages are situated along the paths that wind their way up the slopes of Monteluco, including those of Sant'Isacco, Sant'Antimo and Santa Maria delle Grazie.

Caves in the rocks also provided an ideal shelter for the hermits. It is perhaps thanks to the age-old sacredness of this mountain that its wonderful holm oak woods have been preserved intact.

From the summit of Monteluco, and especially from its Belvedere, wide panoramic views can be enjoyed over the surrounding countryside.

FORTRESS (ROCCA) AND BRIDGE (PONTE DELLE TORRI)

The construction of the impressive Fortress (rocca) dates back to the 14th century, when the Church sent its legate Albornoz to the town in order to quell civil dissent. It was Albornoz who commissioned the building of the fortress by the architect Gattapone and turned it into a symbol of papal authority. During the Renaissance, famous characters such as Lucrezia Borgia and her brother Cesare (the illegitimate children of Pope Alexander VI) stayed there. It was not only a centre of papal power, but also a splendid court: in the 15th century, under Pope Nicholas V,

its interior was transformed and made more luxurious and comfortable. The Fortress has been used for a long time as a prison, but it is now being restructured with a view to using it as a museum and venue for cultural events.

Another superb construction is the *Ponte Delle Torri*, the medieval bridge which joins the hill of Sant'Elia, on which the Fortress stands, and Monteluco. It rests on ten massive arches which span the deep ravine below in a spectacular and impressive piece of engineering. The bridge was almost certainly built before the Fortress, and it is likely that the same architect, Gattapone, was responsible for its design.

THE FESTIVAL OF THE TWO WORLDS

The Festival of the Two Worlds (Festival dei Due Mondi), founded by Giancarlo Menotti in 1958 and held in Spoleto every year in the last few days of June and the first few days of July, may undoubtedly be ranked among the most important and prestigious cultural events to take place annually on the international scene. It offers a series of performances ranging from ballet to opera, from theatre to concerts, all of them of the highest standard and performed, conducted and interpreted by major international artists of long-standing fame. The gala concert held on the final day of the Festival against the magnificent backdrop of the Cathedral is particularly renowned. Special attention is paid during the Festival to avant-garde companies that have succeeded in making an original and important contribution to the performing arts.

So great is the importance and prestige which the Festival enjoys at international level that opera, ballet and theatre buffs, together with lovers of art, flock to Spoleto each year from all over the world.

During the Festival there are also a number of other artistic events, in particular painting and sculpture exhibitions devoted to major international artists. The Festival poster, designed each year by a different artist to advertise the Festival, is also worthy of mention, since the artists chosen for the task are of international standing and in the past have included great names like Mirò, Manzù, Shahn, Capogrossi, Folon and Afro, just to mention a few.

In the last few years, an Arts Festival has been held in the USA along the same lines as the one held in Spoleto, and is a great success.

TERNI

The ancient Interamna Nahartium ("land between two rivers", namely the Nera and the Serra), the birthplace of the Roman emperor Marcus Claudius Tacitus, and perhaps also of the historian Publius Cornelius Tacitus, was also the town which, after the mid-19th century, in common with other Italian cities in the north but almost alone among those in the rest of the Italian peninsula, took an active part in the industrial revolution, which led to a large increase in its population and size, and to considerable economic, social and cultural development. It was known as the "Manchester of Italy".

Although Terni today is mainly a modern industrial town, it preserves part of its historic centre and some fine buildings and churches, including the church of San Francesco (13th century), containing the beautiful Paradisi Chapel with 14th century frescoes; the church of San Salvatore built over the foundations of a Roman Sun Temple; the church of Sant'Alò, a tiny jewel of Romanesque architecture; the church of San Pietro with its interesting apse and cloister; and the Cathedral, built in the 17th century.

Other noteworthy features of the town are the remains of the Roman amphitheatre and of the old walls, and the medieval districts between Via Cavour and Piazza del Duomo, and around Via Garibaldi and Via Roma, where the remains of ancient towers and some fine town-houses can be seen.

The spear of light of A. Pomodoro.

One of Terni's most characteristic monuments is the fountain at the centre of Piazza Tacito. It was reconstructed as a copy of the previous one destroyed by the heavy bombardments which during the Second World War demolished a large part of the town, Terni being a key target for allied bombing raids on account of its many industrial plants and armaments factory.

The basin of the fountain is decorated with a mosaic representing the twelve signs of the Zodiac. At its centre rises a pinnacle of steel: a symbol of the town which boasts one of the most important steelworks in Italy.

Terni can also boast the Basilica of San Valentino which preserves the mortal remains of the Saint to whom it is dedicated: St. Valentine, bishop of Terni, martyred in the 3rd century, and now venerated throughout the world as the patron saint of lovers.

A multimedia centre, the *Bibliomediateca*, has been recently set up in Terni, in the old Town Hall, especially restored and re-organized for this purpose.

Piazza Tacito.

Bibliomediateca.

PALAZZO SPADA

The austere and elegant Palazzo Spada, restored a few years ago to house the Town Hall, dominates Piazza Europa.

It was probably designed by the architect Antonio da Sangallo (who died in Terni in the mid-16th century), but was in large part transformed in the 18th century with the addition of a wing which led to the disappearance of the beautiful garden which characterized the houses of the nobility at that time.

The façade is flanked by two large towers, and consists of a lower storey formed of three large arches and above, three upper rows of windows, of which the central one is the smallest, and a roof-line emphasised by a prominent cornice.

CHURCH OF SAN FRANCESCO (ST. FRANCIS'S)

This beautiful Gothic church was built in 1265, originally following the structure of Franciscan basilicas to be

found throughout Umbria. It later underwent a number of alterations and in particular the addition of two aisles. The façade itself clearly reveals the various phases in its construction: the addition of the two side aisles is clearly detectable, and the difference between the central gothic portal and the two doors on either side of it is quite obvious.

The church suffered considerable damage during the Second World War.

Fortunately, some of its decorations survived the bombardments. Of particular artistic interest is the wonderful *Paradisi Chapel*, decorated with a fine cycle of frescoes painted by Bartolomeo di Tommaso in the 15th century and depicting scenes from the Last Judgement.

The bell-tower erected by Antonio da Orvieto in the 15th century is also handsome.

Palazzo Spada.

CHURCH OF SAN SALVATORE

The church of San Salvatore is one of Terni's most significant monuments not only from an artistic, but also a historical and cultural point of view. In fact, it is built over the foundations of a complex of Roman buildings (probably a domus).

On account of the circular plan of the church, it was long thought that a temple dedicated to the sun god stood on the site, but more thorough research has established that the Roman buildings underneath the church formed part of a Roman house. The church consists of a nave, rectangular in plan, opening out into two chapels, and a circular presbytery. The building of the nave dates to the 12th century, whereas the internal chapels are undoubtedly of a later epoch. The circular area, on the other hand, is of uncertain date, though certainly prior to the rest of the church (theories vary from the 8th to the 11th century).

Well restored to reveal its complex and original structures, the interior as a whole bears the stamp of the traditional Umbrian Romanesque style. It is decorated with various frescoes dating from the 12th to the 15th century.

Cuhrch of San Salvatore.

CATHEDRAL

The Cathedral dominates Piazza del Duomo with its wide and handsome façade. It was built in the mid-17th century over a Romanesque church and even older religious buildings of which the remains can still be seen. The façade rises from a spacious portico while above, the upper part is divided by pilaster strips and windows. A fine series of statues crowns the balcony on top. The interior is 17th century in style, and houses one or two frescoes, an organ designed by Bernini, an altarpiece by Guido Reni and another painting by a Flemish master.

The crypt is of considerable interest: though drastically altered by restoration work in this century, it still preserves its original structure and houses an important series of frescoes. The tomb of Bishop Anastasio is also to be found there, and a few archaeological finds.

Cathedral.

CARSULAE

Carsulae: The excavations.

The interesting archaeological site of Carsulae is situated between Terni and Sangemini. In Roman times Carsulae was an important town, strategically placed on the Via Flaminia which passed through it. Abandoned long ago following an earthquake, it has not yet been excavated fully and further research and studies of the ruins continue today. An interesting complex of monuments may, however, be seen: the area of the *Forum* with the remains of a basilica and two twin temples; the *beautiful arch of San Damiano*, outside which some funeral monuments have been unearthed; and the fairly well-preserved remains of the *theatre* and *amphitheatre*. To one side of the excavations, close to the Forum, is the church of San Damiano, which was built in the medieval period with materials taken from the Roman buildings.

Carsulae: The excavations - View of the theatre.

Next page: View of the lake of Piediluco .

LAKE OF PIEDILUCO

The main road leading from Terni to Rieti climbs steeply, affording fine panoramic views of the basin of Terni below.

After passing the turning for *Miranda* - a charming little town perched on the heights overlooking Terni and set amid pleasant natural scenery - the road runs through *Papigno* and *Marmore* (with its Belvedere looking down on the Waterfalls of the same name), before reaching another of Umbria's enchanting spots: the lake of Piediluco. Peaceful and scenic, the lake, of a rather irregular shape, is surrounded by high tree-covered mountains which give it the appearance of an Alpine lake.

On its banks stands the picturesque little town of Piediluco (its name means "at the foot of the mountain"), with its low houses with their colourful façades crowded into the narrow strip of land between the lake and the mountain.

Facing the town across the lake, with its distinctive cone-like shape, rises Mt. Eco, given its name because it echoes the human voice perfectly. Overlooking the back of the town is the partly ruined but still imposing *Castle* (Rocca), built in its strategic position in the 11th century and fiercely contested by the lords of the surrounding territory.

A popular tourist resort, the lake also provides the setting for international boat races and various water sports. A festival (Festa delle Acque) takes place each year, consisting in a splendid display of allegorical boats on the lake, and in artistic and cultural events in the town.

THE VALLEY OF THE NERA

The Valnerina is the name given to the valley of the River Nera between Terni and Visso. It is a lovely stretch of countryside, with splendid and unspoilt natural scenery. The river makes its way between the wooded slopes of hills and mountains; in parts of the valley it runs through areas of cultivated land, in others it threads its way through narrow gorges with rocky walls. Overlooking the valley are numerous medieval villages, unaltered through the centuries, and the occasional watch-tower, built to guard the road which runs along the bottom of the valley.

MARMORE WATERFALLS

Situated just 7 km from Terni are the famous Marmore Waterfalls (the Cascata delle Marmore), without doubt one of the most spectacular and beautiful natural sights in Italy. It is seldom possible to experience such an awe-inspiring, exceptional spectacle in which power, beauty and motion are combined and blended together: a spectacle which words cannot describe. Suffice it to say that those who see the Marmore Waterfalls will never forget the sight or sound of the foaming mass of the waterfall, crashing with a roar over the rocks and throwing clouds of spray upwards, producing rainbows in the air. The Marmore Waterfalls have been immortalized by great painters such as Corot and by the poet Byron, while they have been visited by princes and famous personalities in every era. The Waterfalls are not entirely a natural phenomenon: they were created by the Roman consul Curius Dentatus in 271 B.C., who built a channel to divert the waters of the River Velino, which stagnated in the higher plain of Rieti, into the River Nera. The waters of the Velino plunge steeply downwards for 165 metres, divided into three leaps of which the first, some 80 metres, is the highest.

Casteldilago: Characteristic view of the Valnerina.

ARRONE

The village is divided into two parts, the more modern Santa Maria and the older part known as "La Terra" ("the Land"). The village is medieval in structure and is famous for trout breeding and for excellent truffles.

FERENTILLO

Made up of two parts named Matterello and Precetto, the village stands in a strategic position guarding the narrow valley of the River Nera, complete with watch-towers and a line of walls climbing up over the ridges of the hills overlooking the village. In the church of Santo Stefano the *"mummies"* are kept, bodies which have been perfectly preserved thanks to the chemical and physical properties of the soil. Rock climbing courses are held on the rocky walls near the village.

ABBEY OF SAN PIETRO IN VALLE

Of enormous historical, cultural and artistic value, both in the development of monasticism and in the development of painting in the transitional phase between the Byzantine and Romanesque periods, the Abbey of San Pietro in Valle was founded in the 8th century by Faraoldo II Duke of Spoleto, who retired to live a monastic life in a spot where some hermits had retired, and where several Roman buildings already stood. The Abbey contains sarcophagi, sculptures and a splendid cycle of frescoes depicting stories from the Old and New Testament.

Above: Arrone
Below: Ferentillo.

NORCIA

Norcia is the main centre of the Nera Valley and is famous for its monuments, for its tourist attractions (it is near the Monti Sibillini and the skiing facilities at Forca Canapine) and as the birthplace of St. Benedict (San Benedetto), patron saint of Europe. St. Benedict lived there between the 5th and 6th century, and founded the Benedictine Order which spread throughout Italy and led to the foundation of a number of monasteries which were involved not only in spreading Christianity but also in economic and cultural activities (their motto was "ora ed labora", pray and work). Santa Scolastica, St. Benedict's sister, was also born at Norcia.

The picturesque Piazza San Benedetto, with its monuments and buildings, marks the centre of the town. In the middle of the square is the *Monument to St. Benedict*; to one side stands the *Castellina*, a fortress built by Vignola in the 16th century for Pope Julius III, which houses a museum. Next to the fortress is the 16th century *Cathedral* (Duomo) with its enormous bell-tower. The square also contains the *church of San Benedetto*, built in the 14th century on the site of an older church which had been built, according to tradition, on the spot where the Saint was born. The church has been altered over the centuries but still has a pleasing façade. The 14th century *Palazzo Comunale* (Town Hall) is also worthy of note, with its fine portico at ground level and open gallery above, and 17th century tower by its side. Among the other monuments in the town we would mention the church of Santa Maria Argentea, the 14th century church of Sant'Agostino, the Gothic church of San Giovanni, the church of the Crucifix and the Oratory of Sant'Agostino. The *Tempietto* is also worth mentioning, a marble building adorned with statues and distinguished by two arches. It dates from the mid-14th century.

Norcia is also famous for its pork products; all over Italy, butchers who are specialized in pork meat, sausages, salamis and hams are called "norcini".

Norcia: Piazza San Benedetto with the Basilica.

PLAINS OF CASTELLUCCIO (PIANI DI CASTELLUCCIO) MT. VETTORE

The Plains of Castelluccio and the Sibillini Mountains (Monti Sibillini) are of great value not only for their natural beauty but also on account of their interesting geological features, and in particular their karst phenomena. The plains are made up of three immense basins surrounded by hills: the Piano Grande (the Large Plain), which is 8 kilometres long, the Piano Piccolo (Small Plain) and the Piano Perduto (Lost Plain). They are approximately 1200 metres high, and are covered in snow for a large part of the year. In Spring and in particular in June, however, they are covered with an exceptional quantity and variety of wild flowers called the "fiorita", which attracts crowds of tourists. The plains are characterized by karst phenomena which have created numerous dolines and cavities in the ground. At one end of the Piano Grande Mt. Vettore towers to a height of 2,475 metres and, on another edge of the plain, the village of *Castelluccio di Norcia* is to be found, famous for its lentils. This village has a typical medieval appearance, with narrow, concentric streets, and presents an original feature: the graffiti with which the walls of its houses are covered, mostly satirical and burlesque in content.

CASCIA

Located close to a loop in the River Corno and dominated by the magnificently rugged peaks of the Umbrian Apennines, Cascia was a town of some importance in the Middle Ages, on account of its position at an important crossroads, and because it was a political, economic and cultural centre for all of the surrounding area.

Today, Cascia is a popular tourist resort, both in summer and winter, and above all is the destination of the many pilgrims who come from all over the world to visit the Sanctuary of St. Rita.

St. Rita was born here towards the end of the 14th century. From girlhood she had a strong religious vocation, but despite her desire to become a nun, was destined to marry, perhaps because this was the wish of her elderly parents. Her married life was, according to tradition, a particularly difficult one. After the violent death of her husband and also of her sons, Rita was granted permission, not without some difficulty, to enter the Convent of the Augustinian Sisters in Cascia. And it was there that she died on 22 May 1457. Her tormented life, the fame of her miracles, and the growing adoration of this exemplary and virtuous woman who soon came to be known as the "Saint of the Impossible", eventually led, though not until this century, to her canonization. Since then devotion to her, and pilgrimages to the places in which she lived, have increased to such an extent that Cascia has become one of the best-loved places for pilgrims from all over the world.

This phenomenon has led to the transformation of the old town in recent times. It has given rise to the building of the Sanctuary and a whole series of hotels, hostels and other facilities to cope with the huge influx of devotees.

In the process some of the town's medieval character has been lost, but fortunately it has kept a few corners in which streets and churches are still preserved to testify to its medieval past.

SANCTUARY OF ST. RITA

The church stands in the centre of medieval Cascia, its façade looking onto the square dedicated to the Saint. It was built between 1937 and 1947 in a mixture of imitation classical, Gothic, Byzantine and Romanesque styles, on a site which had been occupied until then by a little church of medieval origin which had been subjected to various alterations in the course of the centuries.

The interior of the Sanctuary is lavishly decorated with marble sculptures and frescoes depicting episodes from the Saint's life and the miracles she performed. The most interesting part is the Chapel of Saint Rita in which her body lies, clearly visible, in a tomb. The church also contains a relic of the "Body of Christ": the pages of a prayer-book stained with blood by a consecrated host. Next to the Sanctuary is the simple and secluded Augustinian convent in which numerous Christian mementoes are kept.

RELIGIOUS FESTIVITIES AND CEREMONIES

The cult of St. Rita is expressed in the continuous pilgrimages to the Sanctuary - where her body, which has remained intact through the centuries, is displayed in a specially built tomb - and to the places in which she lived and worked. The pilgrimages never cease throughout the whole year, but the greatest homage to the Saint is paid on 22 May, the anniversary of her death. On this occasion the religious ceremonies are particularly solemn; apart from the religious services held in the Church of St. Rita and in other sacred places, the festivity has its focal point in a touching enactment of the life of the Saint and especially of her most famous miracles. These are represented in medieval costumes in the square in front of the Sanctuary. The rite is also accompanied by the *distribution of blessed roses*. But the most evocative moment of the ceremony is perhaps the extraordinary torchlight parade that lights up the whole of the town of Cascia during the night between the 21 and 22 May. It is called by a particularly suggestive name: the *Fire of Faith*. A procession of lights symbolizing the passage of St. Rita from earthly to supernatural life, accompanies her in her journey, and the light from the torches seems to recall the radiance of her soul.

The flame that lights the torches is brought every year from Lourdes, twinned with Cascia on account of the religious associations and traditions which the two towns have in common.

A festivity is held each year in the village of Roccaporena, on the third Sunday of June, with the distribution of the blessed roses which were so dear to the Saint and which are her symbol, and for which she has been called the "Rose of Roccaporena".

We should also mention the religious services which take place in Cascia during Holy Week and in particular the moving procession of the Dead Christ.

ROCCAPORENA

About 6 km from Cascia, situated on top of the heights overlooking the town, Roccaporena stands in a magnificent position, commanding wonderful panoramic views of the surrounding countryside.

It is in this village that the memories of the Saint are most vivid.

It is here that her home is situated; it has now been transformed into a small chapel, a simple, quiet place of worship, evocative of the memory of the Saint. Here, too, is situated the 14th century church of San Montano in which she was married and besides which another Sanctuary dedicated to her, and a Pilgrims Centre have since been built. Another site of particular interest for those who go to Roccaporena on pilgrimage is the *Rock of Saint Rita*, which rises, proud and solitary, over the village itself. According to tradition, it was to this solitary place that Rita would withdraw to pray so often and for such long periods that the rock has been made smooth by her knees.

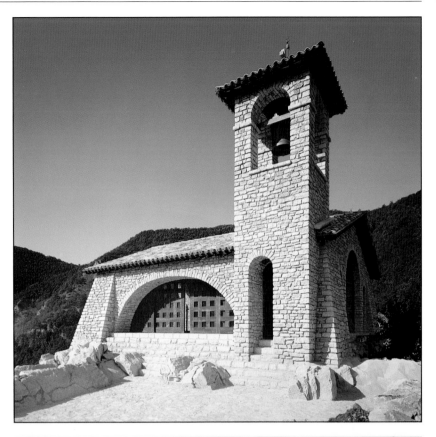

Exterior and interior of the Chapel on the Rock of St. Rita.

NARNI

A town of great artistic interest, situated along the Via Flaminia a few kilometres from Terni, Narni stands in a picturesque position on a hill overlooking the valley of the River Nera. The town is perched on a rocky spur and is dominated by the impressive fortress built by Albornoz. Narni has ancient origins; founded by the Umbrians with the name of Nequinum, when it was conquered by the Romans it was rechristened Narnia. Under Rome it grew in importance and influence thanks to its strategic position: evidence of this can be seen in the superb Roman bridge of which part of the structure and one enormous arch still remain. Later, Narni suffered the barbaric invasions and fell to the Lombards before becoming a city-state in the Middle Ages, when it extended its dominion over a vast area of land. From the 14th century onwards it was controlled by a series of lords until Albornoz annexed it to the Papal States.

It was the home of the Roman emperor Nerva and the condottiere Erasmo Gattamelata.

The town has kept its medieval appearance, and most of its monuments date from medieval times.

The *Cathedral*, dedicated to San Giovenale, is an interesting Romanesque building containing a chapel to the Saint dating from the 9th century, and works of art by Vecchietta, Mezzastris and Torresani.

Piazza dei Priori is a gem of medieval architecture, containing: the 14th century *Loggia dei Priori*, with its powerful arches, perhaps designed by Gattapone; the *Pulpit* of the town-criers; the *Palazzo del Podestà* (the Governors' Palace), now the Town Hall, built between the 12th and 15th centuries, housing Roman finds and paintings by Ghirlandaio and Gozzoli; and the simple and graceful *fountain*.

Another gem is the tiny *church of Santa Maria in Pensole,* with its low portico and elegant doorways. The *churches of San Domenico* and *San*

Francesco are also of interest. The charm of Narni, however, lies in its narrow streets, its little squares and the archways between its houses, which create the town's delightful atmosphere.

The recently restored *fortress* (Rocca), commissioned by Albornoz as a symbol of Papal control over the area, dominates the town.

On the outskirts stand the remains of the Roman *bridge of Augustus*, with its one remaining arch of enormous proportions, which shows us how impressive the bridge must have been when intact, and how solidly it was built.

On the hill facing the bridge stands the *Abbey of San Cassiano*.

An important festival takes place every year in Narni, on the anniversary of the town's patron saint: the Ring Race (Corsa dell'Anello), a contest among three competitors on horseback, representing the three districts into which the town is divided. At the same time, the town organizes processions in medieval costumes, cultural events and banquets with local gastronomic products, held in the medieval-style taverns opened especially for the occasion.

The *Franciscan Monastery of the Cave of Sant'Urbano* is situated a few kilometres away from Narni. Set in a dense wood of holm oak and chestnut trees, the monastery complex is in a quiet, tranquil spot, permeated with the simple, spiritual atmosphere which characterizes all Franciscan hermitages. The complex consists of a monastery, two small churches, a cloister, a refectory and a number of other rooms. The monks' cells are built against the rocks; the original church is a tiny room; in one of the cells St. Francis's bed can still be seen. Near the complex are grottoes in which St. Francis liked to retire to pray. There is a lovely view from the cloister.

Page 110: Above: Panorama.
Below: The fortress.
On this page:
Above: Abbey of San Cassiano.
Below: Franciscan Monastery of
the Cave of Sant'Urbano - Cloister.

ORVIETO

Many are the factors which make Orvieto one of the finest and most interesting towns in Italy: firstly, its glorious artistic heritage, including not only the glittering splendour of its Cathedral but also the remains of ancient civilizations such as that of the Etruscans and secondly, its incomparable position on a high plateau of tufa rock, rising over the surrounding countryside like an island emerging from an emerald sea. The town is typically medieval and this adds another picturesque and suggestive note to the whole. Nor should we forget the other factors which have contributed to the fame of this city: its justly renowned wines, its local traditions, the ceremonies of Corpus Christi and the Palombella, and all those handicrafts which have been passed down from the distant past and have become art forms in their own right, such as ceramics and lace-making.

There is still controversy over the origins of Orvieto. It is certain, however, that at some point the Etruscans settled in this area, and in particular on the rocky plateau on which the town stands, the evidence being in the large necropolis found nearby.

The town was conquered by the Romans, but it was not until the barbarian invasions, under which it suffered particularly gruelling hardships, that we have more certain information about its history.

In the 11th century Orvieto became an independent city-state and acquired growing importance, not only extending its rule over much of the surrounding territory, but acquiring all those monuments that still distinguish it in so unmistakeable a way today. Long torn by civil strife - the struggles between the rival factions of the Filippeschi and Monaldeschi - Orvieto was eventually annexed to the Papal States in the 15th century.

CATHEDRAL

The Cathedral is one of the most splendid achievements of medieval

art in Italy: a majestic and unforgettable sight. It was built to celebrate the Miracle of the Corporal (or chalice-cloth) which occurred in 1263 and to provide a fitting shrine for its relic. The story goes that a priest, in doubt as to the real presence of the Body of Christ in the consecrated Host, on celebrating Mass at Bolsena on his return from a pilgrimage to Rome, saw blood dripping from the Host which was staining the Corporal. Informed of the miracle, Pope Urban IV, who then resided at Orvieto, established the feast of Corpus Christi, the "body of Christ", and later it was decided to build a shrine to house the precious relic and to commemorate the miracle in a fitting manner. The building of the Cathedral began at the end of the 13th century. The initial design was by Fra' Bevignate da Perugia and later Uguccione da Orvieto. But so many changes were subsequently made to their plans that the foundations and supporting framework of the building began to be less safe than was desirable, and the architect Lorenzo Maitani was called in to complete the work and make the necessary adjustments to ensure the stability of the building. In fact, Maitani made a decisive contribution to the structure of the church but many other artists, of course, contributed to the completion of this ambitious building.

Indeed, the history of its construction would require a more detailed study than is possible here. What must be said, however, is that, in spite of the various contributions by so many different artists, the Cathedral of Orvieto presents an exceptionally harmonious appearance. The boldness of its architectural forms, the beauty of its paintings and the delicate polychromy of its different kinds of marble are aesthetically blended into an inseparable whole: a unique, unforgettable and moving sight.

The façade is an exceptional jewel of Gothic architecture. It has the form of a large, richly-ornamented polyptych composed of many panels in which a series of sculptures, bas-reliefs and mosaics of the most varied subjects are harmoniously inserted. The polychromy of the different kinds of marble and the gilding of the mosaics are particularly striking: the whole façade seems to glitter and sparkle with their brilliance.

The interior of the Cathedral is magnificent and full of masterpieces of painting and sculpture. We may note in particular the *Chapel of the Corporal* (Cappella del Corporale) in which the precious blood-stained chalice-cloth described above is kept. Its walls and vaults are decorated with frescoes by Pietro Lorenzetti and Gentile Fabriano. A frescoed Madonna and Child by Gentile da Fabriano

can be seen in the left aisle, close to the baptismal font, while in the left transept there is a fine Pietà - or Deposition - the work of the Orvieto sculptor Ippolito Scalza. This perfect group of four life-sized figures is carved from a single block of marble. The artist apparently began it in 1570 and worked on it for nine years, eventually completing and signing it in 1579. Magnificent, too, is the *Chapel of San Brizio*, decorated with a superb cycle of frescoes by Luca Signorelli. This Chapel with a Gothic vaulted ceiling is protected by a splendid wrought-iron gate. The history of its decoration is complicated: it was begun in 1447 by Fra Giovanni da Fiesole, better known as Beato Angelico, who left Orvieto after completing only two vaults and never returned. Other artists of the time, such as Benozzo Gozzoli and Perugino, were invited in vain to continue his work, and it was not until 1489 that the work was resumed by Luca Signorelli, who completed the vaults following Beato Angelico's sketches and then frescoed the other walls of the Chapel. He enriched the work with such episodes as "Stories of the Antichrist", " The End of the World" and the "Prophecies". Such was the force and expressiveness of his frescoes that they later inspired no less than Michelangelo for some parts of the Sistine Chapel.

PALAZZO SOLIANO (FORMER PALAZZO DEI PAPI OR PALACE OF THE POPES)

Built in the Gothic style, this handsome and monumental building in tufa stands to the right of the Cathedral. It was begun by Pope Boniface VIII in 1297. Work was then interrupted, only to resume again in 1443. It was restored in 1896 by the architect Paolo Zampi who added the windows in the upper storey and the battlements. Today the Palazzo Soliano houses the Cathedral Museum (Museo dell'Opera del Duomo). Under the porticoes are three Roman arches, various inscriptions and milestones. The monumental external staircase leads up to the hall in which various frescoes removed from churches in Orvieto are displayed, together with a number of valuable sculptures and paintings from the 13th and 14th century, including a wonderful polyptych by Simone Martini, statues by the Pisano family and several works in enamelled terracotta by the Della Robbia family.

PALAZZO DEL CAPITANO DEL POPOLO

An imposing building in tufa, begun in the 12th and completed in the 13th century, it is built in a composite Romanesque-Gothic style. The series of massive arches on the ground floor and the character given to the building by the cornices are particularly striking. The three-mullioned windows and the decorations which embellish the building are of considerable elegance. In recent times the architects Paolo and Carlo Zampi have restored the building carefully reconstructing the damaged parts and restoring the original forms.

Above: Palazzo del Capitano del Popolo.

Below: Palazzo Soliano.

WELL OF SAN PATRIZIO

The designer of this highly original well was Antonio da Sangallo the Younger. He built it, beginning in 1527, at the request of Pope Clement VII, who lived in Orvieto at the time. Its purpose was to provide the city with a water supply in the event of siege. Cylindrical in shape, it is 62 metres deep and contains two concentric spiral flights of steps designed in such a way as to prevent those going down from obstructing those going up. Each flight of steps consists of 248 wide steps to enable pack-animals, as well as people, to use them. Numerous windows provide them with air and light. The well is a formidable piece of engineering, and to go down into it is a fascinating experience: as we gradually approach the bottom, the light changes, the temperature drops and everything seems to assume different shapes and colours. Peering upwards through the windows, continually changing optical effects are created; at the same time both the descent and ascent appear interminable, step after step along the seemingly endless spiral staircase.

The Well of San Patrizio.

The Abbey of SS. Severo and Martirio.

ABBEY OF SAINTS SEVERO AND MARTIRIO

This abbey complex just outside Orvieto is of considerable interest. Originally built in the 12th century, it belonged first to the Benedictines and later to the French Order of the Premonstratensian Canons who enlarged it, constructing a large refectory, a cloister (now destroyed), and a chapter hall in Romanesque-Gothic style. But perhaps the most impressive part of the abbey today is its massive twelve-sided bell-tower, whose battlements form a kind of coronet. The whole complex is permeated with a simple and mystic atmosphere, while the views from the abbey of the surrounding territory are lovely.

FEAST OF THE PALOMBELLA

Against the picturesque background of its squares and monuments, Orvieto is the scene each year of interesting cultural and religious events, such as the Feasts of the Palombella, of Corpus Christi and of the Assumption, and the Trade Fair of Umbrian wines and local handicrafts.

The Feast of the Palombella was instituted in the 14th century and is celebrated in front of the Cathedral on Whit Sunday, at midday. A tabernacle with the figures of Mary and the Apostles is placed in front of the central doorway of the Cathedral. A wire is stretched between the tabernacle and the lantern on the church of San Francesco on the Via Maitani opposite the Cathedral; when the bishop gives the order, a model of a white dove - the Palombella - slides swiftly down this wire to the tabernacle, where it triggers off an explosion of fireworks and lights up little flames over the heads of the Virgin and the Apostles. From the outcome of the ceremony people used to draw good or bad omens for the agricultural produce of the current year. According to a long-standing custom, the dove is presented by the bishop to the most recent bride in the town.

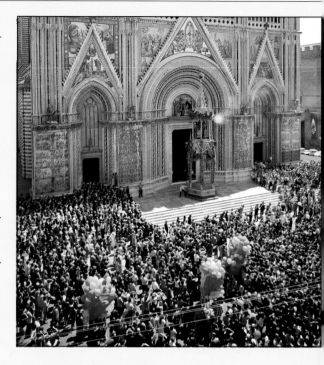

FEAST OF CORPUS CHRISTI

Established by Pope Urban IV in Orvieto in 1264, the Feast of Corpus Christi is celebrated each year with particular solemnity, with the relics of the Miracle of Bolsena, kept in the Cathedral, carried in procession through the streets of Orvieto, accompanied by some 300 representatives of the various districts of the town dressed in magnificent medieval costumes.

TODI

One of the most beautiful towns in Umbria and in the whole of Italy, Todi stands out for its beautiful hilltop position, its enchanting medieval atmosphere and its many historical monuments. It has recently been designated as the "ideal town".

According to a legend regarding the origins of Todi, an eagle indicated the hill on which the town was to arise, and in fact the eagle became its coat of arms.

Todi was originally an Etruscan town but was in close contact with the Umbrians who settled on the opposite bank of the Tiber. Later conquered by the Romans, it came to acquire considerable importance and was awarded the name "Marzia" as a result of the courage in battle displayed by its citizens during the wars which it fought on the side of Rome.

In the Middle Ages it became an independent city-state, growing in prosperity, and extending so much that it had to erect a new, broader circuit of walls (the previous ones were Etruscan and Roman). It was during this period that most of the monumental buildings still standing in the centre of Todi were built.

It was later ruled by various lords until it eventually became part of the Papal States and, after 1860, of the Kingdom of Italy. Todi was the birthplace of the famous poet of Franciscan lauds, Jacopone da Todi (born in 1230), a man devoted to a life of severe penance. He was thrown into prison for having opposed Pope Boniface VIII and ended his days in terrible torments.

A visit to the town is of the greatest interest for the beauty of its monuments and its medieval centre. Two circles of walls (one Etruscan-Roman, the other medieval) still enclose the town which occupies the summit and slopes of a hill.

Important cultural and artistic events are held in Todi every year.

PIAZZA DEL POPOLO

Occupying the heart of Todi, at the highest point of the hill on which the town stands, Piazza del Popolo is justly considered one of the most beautiful squares in Italy.

Built over the area once occupied by the ancient Roman Forum, it is rectangular in shape and is surrounded by magnificent buildings, including the Cathedral, the Palazzo dei Priori, the Palazzo del Popolo and the Palazzo del Capitano.

The side of the square facing the Cathedral is occupied by the *Palazzo dei Priori*, built in the 14th century. Though partly altered in subsequent centuries, it still preserves its original aspect.

It is distinguished by a beautiful 14th century tower which retains its original trapezial structure. On one of the longer sides of the square, the *Palazzo del Popolo* and *Palazzo del Capitano* stand side by side.

The former, built in the 13th century, has a portico supported on low arches at ground floor level and fine crenellated battlements.

The Palazzo del Capitano is distinguished by a broad diagonal staircase resting on a low arch, and its façade is adorned with elegant mullioned windows with three and four lights. The interior of the Palazzo del Capitano houses a Picture Gallery and Archaeological Museum.

The Gallery contains a number of valuable paintings, including some by the Umbrian painter Lo Spagna; the Museum houses archaeological finds from the Todi area dating from the Etruscan and Roman periods. Of particular interest are the Sala del Consiglio Generale - the Council Hall - and the Sala del Capitano del Popolo - the Hall of the Representative of the People - with traces of sculptures and paintings dating back to the 13th century.

CATHEDRAL

Superbly situated on top of a broad flight of steps at the northern end of Piazza del Popolo, the Cathedral (or Duomo) provides an incomparable finishing touch to this magnificent

Piazza del Popolo.

The façade of the Cathedral.

monumental square. The building dates back to the early 12th century, but has undergone a number of alterations and embellishments in various periods. During the period of Roman rule the site on which it stands was occupied by one of the buildings surrounding the central area of the Forum, perhaps a temple.

The façade of the Cathedral is particularly interesting and beautiful: rectangular in shape, it is divided up by pilaster strips and adorned by three rose-windows and three doorways, the central one being especially remarkable for the gracefulness of its lines and the delicacy of its decorations. The harmonious interior, divided into a nave and aisles by pillars and columns decorated with wonderful capitals, contains several interesting paintings.

A visit to the Cathedral may also include the crypt below the presbytery and a walk round the outside of the building to admire the magnificent and complex architecture of the apse; this retains its original Romanesque forms, whereas the rest of the building is mainly distinguished by alterations in the Gothic style.

THE CHURCH OF SAN FORTUNATO

The church is reached from the Piazza del Popolo by taking the Via Mazzini to the side of the Palazzo dei Priori. We pass some interesting medieval buildings and then the fine Teatro Comunale, before coming to the Piazza Jacopone da Todi (where the poet's monument stands) and then the Piazza della Repubblica, where a stairway mounts a gently sloping hill to the church above. The fusion between nature and architecture adds to the beauty of its elegant façade.

Gothic in style and built in the 15th century - whereas the rest of the building was begun in the 13th - this is notable for its magnificent portal, decorated by a frame of delicately carved mouldings and colonnettes.

The interior, too, is elegant and notable for its slender, luminous and spacious architectural structure. It contains the tomb of the early Franciscan poet Jacopone da Todi and some fine paintings and statues, including a beautiful "Madonna and Child" by the early 15th century Florentine artist Masolino da Panicale and some frescoes of Giotto which decorate part of the side chapels.

The Hight Altar and the finely-carved choir stalls date to the 14th century.

The Church of San Fortunato.

CHURCH OF SANTA MARIA DELLA CONSOLAZIONE

Situated on the outskirts of Todi, outside the town walls, the Renaissance church of Santa Maria della Consolazione stands in splendid isolation in the green countryside, overlooking the valley below. The design of the church has been attributed to the architect Bramante, the great Renaissance artist who mainly worked in Rome. Though not supported by any official documents, the attribution to him is virtually certain, since his name has been associated with the church since the 16th century and particularly because his hand is clearly detectable in the overall structure and style of the building.

It is equally clear that Renaissance architects of great fame and talent such as Sangallo, Vignola and Peruzzi, also contributed to the design of the church. It is beyond dispute, however, that the church of Santa Maria della Consolazione is one of the finest and most harmonious examples of Renaissance art in the whole of Italy and, as far as Umbria is concerned, one of the rare examples of the architecture of this period to be found in the region.

The church is built in the form of a Greek cross, with many-sided apses which are united in the dome.

The interior is majestic, serene, harmonious and well-proportioned. A series of statues of the Apostles are placed in the niches around the walls. A fresco depicting "Our Lady of Consolation" is placed over the main altar.

Above: Santa Maria della Consolazione - Dome.
Below: Santa Maria della Consolazione - Interior with baroque altar.
Next page: Santa Maria della Consolazione.

PHOTOGRAPHS:

Archivio Plurigraf

A.P.T. Città di Castello: 33 Above.

Marka: 4/5 - 8/9 - 40/41 - 44/45 - 68 - 78/79 - 86/87 - 100: G. Simeone.

Marka: 23 - 25 - 88 - 90 Above - 90 Below: T. Conti.

Marka: 27 - 28 - 29 - 30 Above - 30 Below - 31 - 32 - 33 Above - 80 - 82 Above
82 Below - 83 - 96 Below - 104/105 - 114 -115: D. Donadoni.

Marka: 91: V. Arcomano.

Foto Lucarini: 92 Above.

Foto De Furia: 92 Below.

M. Sabatini: 13 Below.

M. Santarelli: 110 Below - 111 Above.

S. Svizzeretto: 99 - 101 - 102 Above - 102 Below.

F. Tulli: 93 - 94 Above - 94 Below - 95 Above - 95 Below - 96 Above.

The aerial views have been authorized by S.M.A. (402 - 16/5/91 and 506 - 20/6/91).

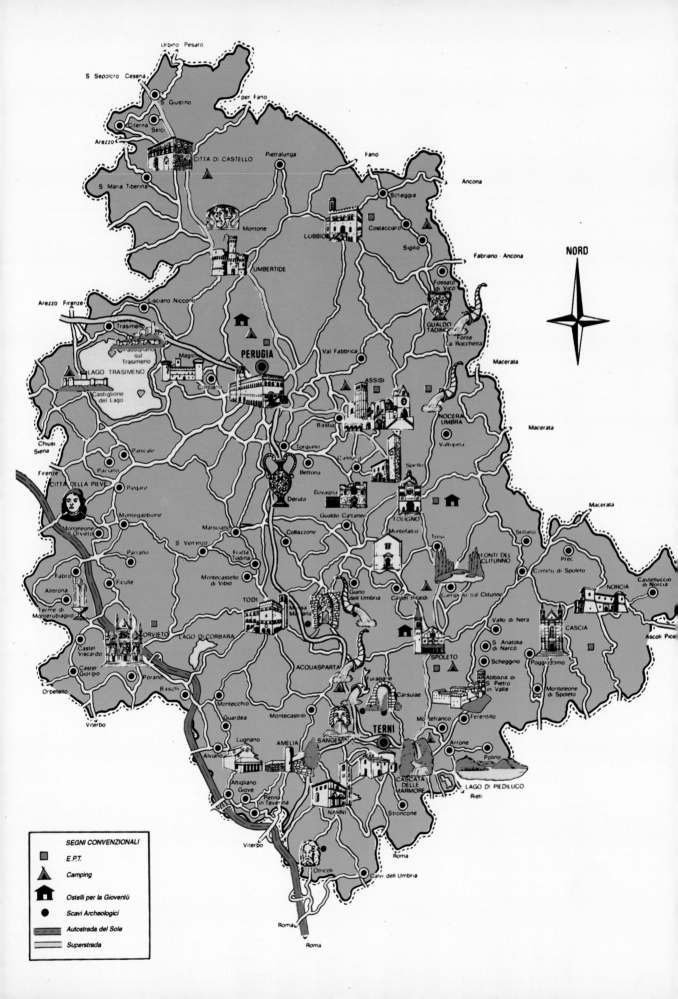

NORD

PERUGIA

CITTÀ DI CASTELLO

Urbino Pesaro
S Sepolcro Cesena
S Giustino
Citerna Selci
Arezzo
S Maria Tiberina
per Fano
Pietralunga
Fano
Ancona
Scheggia
Montone
Costacciaro
GUBBIO
Sigillo
Fabriano · Ancona
UMBERTIDE
Fossato
di Vico
GUALDO
TADINO
Fonte
La Rocchetta
Lisciano Niccone
Macerata
Arezzo Firenze
Trasimeno
Val Fabbrica
Passignano
sul
Trasimeno
Magione
ASSISI
LAGO TRASIMENO
Corciano
NOCERA
UMBRA
Castiglione
del Lago
Bastia
Valtopina
Macerata
Chiusi
Siena
Torgiano
Cannara
Spello
Panicale
Bettona
Firenze
Paciano
Bevagna
FOLIGNO
CITTÀ DELLA PIEVE
Piegaro
Deruta
Gualdo Cattaneo
Sellano
Montegabbione
Marsciano
Montefalco
Trevi
Prec
Monteleone
d'Orvieto
S Venanzo
Collazzone
FONTI DEL
CLITUNNO
Cerreto di Spoleto
Parrano
Fratta
Todina
Giano
dell'Umbria
Castel Ritaldi
Campello sul Clitunno
NORCIA
Castelluccio
di Norcia
Fabro
Ficulle
Montecastello
di Vibio
TODI
Massa
Martana
Vallo di Nera
CASCIA
Allerona
Terme di
Monterubiaglio
Castel
Viscardo
ORVIETO
LAGO DI CORBARA
S Anatolia
di Narco
Scheggino
Poggiodomo
Orbetello
Castel
Giorgio
Porano
Baschi
ACQUASPARTA
SPOLETO
Abbazia di
S Pietro
in Valle
Monteleone
di Spoleto
Ascoli Piceno
Furapane
Carsulae
Montecchio
Guardea
Montecastrilli
Montefranco
Ferentillo
Viterbo
Lugnano
AMELIA
SANGEMINI
TERNI
Arrone
Polino
Alviano
CASCATA
DELLE
MARMORE
LAGO DI PIEDILUCO
Rieti
Attigliano
Giove
Penna
in Teverina
NARNI
Stroncone
Viterbo
Roma
Otricoli
Calvi dell'Umbria
Roma
Roma